The **Myth**
of the
Nice Girl

Contents

To my formal and informal mentors . . .
I'm forever grateful for your incredible wisdom and
invaluable advice. It's my honor to pay it forward.

For information about permission to reproduce selections
from this book, write to trade.permissions@hmhco.com or to
Permissions, Houghton Mifflin Harcourt Publishing Company,
3 Park Avenue, 19th Floor, New York, New York 10016.

hmhco.com

Library of Congress Cataloging-in-Publication Data
Names: Hauser, Fran, author.
Title: The myth of the nice girl : achieving a career you love without
becoming a person you hate / Fran Hauser.
Description: Boston : Houghton Mifflin Harcourt, 2018. | Includes
bibliographical references and index.
Identifiers: LCCN 2017046069 (print) | LCCN 2017054639 (ebook) |
ISBN 9781328832979 (ebook) | ISBN 9781328832955 (hardcover)
Subjects: LCSH: Women—Vocational guidance. | Career development. |
Assertiveness in women. | Success in business.
Classification: LCC HF5382.6 (ebook) | LCC HF5382.6 .H375 2018 (print) |
DDC 650.1—dc23
LC record available at https://lccn.loc.gov/2017046069

Book design by Chrissy Kurpeski
Typeset in ITC Century Std

Printed in the United States of America
DOC 10 9 8 7 6 5 4
4500740343

Out of respect for their privacy, I have changed the names and
characterizing details of some of the people who appear in these pages.

The Myth
of the
Nice Girl

Achieving a Career You
Love
Without Becoming a Person You
Hate

FRAN HAUSER
with Jodi Lipper

Houghton Mifflin Harcourt
Boston   New York

Author's Note

The one question I've been asked the most over the course of my career is, "How can you be so nice . . . and still be successful?"

It first struck me that this is a real issue that women struggle with when I was president of digital for *People* magazine back in 2009. So many of the women I worked with and mentored wanted to better understand how I had risen to that leadership position while having a reputation for being so nice.

I came to realize that many of these young women were convinced that they had to somehow suppress their "niceness" to get ahead. They were worried—and sometimes rightly so—that if they acted kindly and collaboratively at work, they'd be labeled as "too nice." The ongoing myth of the "nice girl" is that she's weak, a pushover, a "people pleaser," and clearly not someone who is a natural leader or super effective at her job. At the same time, these women were concerned that if they voiced their opinions, stood up for themselves, and put their own ambition first, they'd end up in another box, this one labeled "bitch." One after another, women asked me how they could find the perfect balance between being nice and being strong at work.

The truth is that it's taken me years to find my own balance, and it's something I still struggle with from time to time. When I was in my twenties, I received advice from bosses and mentors to act tougher and to develop a harder edge. "Fran, you're too nice," they told me. "You need to toughen up, or people will walk all over you." I bought into this myth and tried stifling my empathy and kindness, but the truth was, behaving that way just wasn't me. It felt fake and inauthentic. Plus, I saw that it wasn't as effective for my career as using kindness had been.

After years of self-discovery, building a successful career, and paying close attention to what worked and—most importantly— what felt right for me, I ultimately came to see that I didn't have to sacrifice my values or hide my authentic personality in the name of achieving success. In fact, as I learned to own my natural kindness, it has become my professional superpower. It has helped me build my personal confidence; the loyalty of those who've worked with me; and a strong, trusting, faithful network of colleagues, mentors, and mentees. I fully believe it can do the same things for you.

Over the past eight years, I've had thousands of conversations about this topic with women—one-on-one, via social media and digital mentoring platforms, and through speaking engagements. I've shared my own experiences, as well as the insights from my various mentors and colleagues. Back in 2009, I also did some research to see what resources were available for all the women who were facing this same issue. But what I found was disappointing: no business guides seemed to regard being nice as powerful at all. In fact, too many books still put forward the myth that "nice girls" can't get the corner office or become respected leaders. That was when I realized that there was a need for this book.

Then, my life took a turn. Our first son, Anthony, came into our lives in 2010 and our second son, Will, followed in 2011. Between being a mom and having a demanding career, my life was overflowing. So I pressed pause on writing the book. Then, in 2014, I took the scary and thrilling step of creating a new career for myself. I left media and moved into startup investing. When I saw just how much my network helped support me in that career transition, I started thinking seriously about the book again.

The breakthrough moment for me was a blog post I wrote for Forbes.com in January 2016, entitled "How Nice Women Can Finish First When They Ask the Right Questions." It really struck a chord with readers and became one of the most popular posts in Denise Restauri's Mentoring Moments series. I was suddenly overwhelmed with women reaching out to me through Facebook, Twitter, and email. That was when I knew that not only was there still a need for this book, but that I had to write it.

While I've received very strong support for the book in many circles, I've also received pushback from others. The word "nice" is emotionally loaded for many women; some have an immediate, adverse reaction to it. I fully understand that, and it's precisely why I want to "rebrand" the idea of a "nice girl" as someone who is not meek or a people pleaser, but who uses her authentic kindness to sidestep regressive stereotypes about what a strong leader looks like. There is real power hidden in traits like empathy, kindness, and compassion that are undervalued in the business world. When coupled with an appropriate dose of savvy and ambition, these overlooked superpowers can help launch your career to the top.

In these pages, you will discover the principles that have allowed me and hundreds of other strong, kind women to rise above double standards and thrive in the workforce. *The Myth of the Nice Girl* will show you how to negotiate powerfully, to speak up so people listen, to project confidence, to own your decisions, and to deal with conflict—all while never hiding the nice woman you know yourself to be. When you reject the outdated playbook that says you must be ruthless in order to succeed in business and instead learn how to harness the untapped strength of kindness, your power to achieve your dreams and goals will be unstoppable.

Fran Hauser
Summer 2017

The **Myth**
of the
Nice Girl

1

Nice Is Your Superpower

WHEN I WAS IN MY EARLY TWENTIES, I WAS working at Ernst & Young, one of the biggest professional services firms in the world. I was young, ambitious, and extremely hard working, and I was doing well in my role there, but I was also getting a lot of feedback from my boss about specific things I needed to work on.

For example, one of the companies my team was assigned to service was Coca-Cola Bottling Company of New York. I was the youngest person on the team and felt incredibly intimidated by one of the vice presidents at Coke, who was an imposing older man. In our meetings, I found myself constantly nodding and agreeing to pretty much everything he and the other people in the room said; I was just too nervous to speak up and voice my own opinions. Either that or I uttered a noncommittal "That's interesting," no matter what subject was being discussed. We could have been talking about what to get for lunch, and if someone had suggested sushi, my response would have been, "That's interesting."

I just didn't want to make waves or create any conflict by voicing a strong opinion one way or the other. It was my way of show-

ing interest and being a part of the conversation while always trying to remain agreeable. But looking back on this, I can't help but
laugh at myself. Who knew that sushi could be so interesting?

One day, after one of these meetings, my boss pulled me aside.
"Fran, you're yessing the client to death," he told me. "It's okay to
push back sometimes if you do it respectfully. It actually makes
you less interesting to just say 'yes' or 'that's interesting' all the
time. You need to start saying something more significant and sharing your opinions."

This was the first time I realized that I was trying to be too much
of a "people pleaser" at work. By hiding behind a façade of agree-
ableness, I was hijacking my own effectiveness. Of course I had my
own opinions and ideas, but I had been waiting for permission to
share them. And now I had it.

In the next meeting, the client made a suggestion about changing how we disclosed certain information on the quarterly financial
statements. I thought it was a great idea, but I wasn't sure that we
could make the change and still meet our deadline for that quarter.
Feeling nervous and with my voice probably quieter than it should
have been, I said, "Why don't we implement that change in the next
quarter so we can make sure to meet this quarter's deadline?"

After I spoke, I looked up at the client nervously, afraid that he
would think my comment was stupid or off-putting. "That's a good
point," he said simply, and I breathed a huge sigh of relief.

Over the coming weeks, I started speaking up more and more,
and I grew increasingly comfortable with voicing my thoughts. I
knew it was working a few weeks later when the client stopped at
my cube after a meeting and actually asked for my opinion about
something. He had never done this before. I realized that by sharing my opinions on a more regular basis in our meetings, I'd proven
to him that my thoughts had value.

This was a big step in the right direction, but I was still getting
some negative pushback about my relationships with people in-

house. I was spending a lot of time trying to get my colleagues' buy-in before making a decision, and I had a mentor who kept encouraging me to toughen up and stop worrying so much about what other people thought.

I had a colleague named Jane who was responsible for giving approval for the proposals we sent out to clients. Jane was notorious for taking her time with her approvals, and she always gave me a hard time, especially when I approached her with a tight deadline. Normally, I did my best to accommodate her, but when my boss came to me with a new proposal that he needed to send right away, I was torn. My gut told me to go to Jane and just honestly explain the situation, but I kept hearing my mentor's voice in my ear telling me to be tougher and to stop worrying about getting other people's buy-in.

Finally, I decided to go above Jane's head to her boss, Eric. I knew he would understand the urgency and give me the approval I needed without asking too many questions. And he did. My boss was pleased, my mentor approved, and the proposal was a win. But knowing how I had bypassed Jane, I didn't feel right about the way I'd gotten that win.

I asked myself how I would have felt if someone treated me in the same way I'd treated Jane, and the answer was "not good." I had disenfranchised her by going above her head. And, sure enough, that ill-gotten win came back to haunt me the very next time I needed approval from Jane: she said no. I went back to Eric, but he told me, "I'm sorry, Fran, but you need to work with Jane on this one."

Deep down, I knew he was right. I couldn't keep going above Jane's head. I needed to find a way to work with her. But at this point, I was so confused about how to go about it. Should I go with my instincts to be nice and accommodating . . . or double down on my new tough approach that had gotten me the results I wanted last time?

Feeling torn, I thought back to my original role model and source of inspiration: my mother. She was an Italian immigrant (my family moved to the United States when I was two years old) with four children when she opened a tailoring shop in Mount Kisco, New York, in the 1970s. Her English was broken, and she didn't have any professional training, but she managed to become a successful small businesswoman. This was thanks in part to her skills, but mostly due to her personality. She was always incredibly kind and loving to her clients, and they absolutely adored her for it.

My father was the same way. A stonemason who served mostly wealthy local clients, he was (and still is) one of the most beloved members of our community. My parents' clients were always loyal and incredibly giving to my family. They gave us bags of hand-me-down designer clothing, let us use their swimming pools in the summer, and one of them even sold me my first car—a 1970s baby blue Fiat with no power steering—for just a few hundred dollars. But it wasn't just about generously sharing their wealth with us; these people genuinely liked and respected my parents because they were so nice.

I thought about my situation with Jane and asked myself what my parents would have done in a similar situation. While I was trying to succeed in the corporate world rather than in a tailoring or stonemasonry business, it was important to me to develop the same types of relationships with colleagues and clients that my parents had with theirs—and to do it in a way that I felt good about.

I went to Jane the next day and asked her out to lunch. She hesitantly agreed, and as soon as we sat down, I apologized straight from the heart. "Jane," I told her, "I really messed up." I explained the pressure I was feeling to deliver a fast "yes" to my boss. "Knowing how quickly we needed the proposal turned around, I felt in the moment that it would be best to go to Eric right away," I said, "but I realized after the fact that I disrespected you and didn't give you a chance. I'm so sorry, and I promise that, going forward, this will never happen again."

I could see a wave of relief come over Jane, and she graciously accepted my apology. For the rest of our time at lunch, I took advantage of the opportunity to get to know her a little better. I learned that she had two young girls, and when I asked to see pictures of them, Jane's face completely lit up. This was a lovely side of her that I'd never seen before—a side of her that I'd never given myself an opportunity to see.

I stayed true to my promise to never again go above Jane's head. But more important, I was never even tempted to. Jane and I developed a great working relationship. Whenever I needed something from her, I made sure to go to her first. I also frequently went out of my way to touch base with her and ask about her daughters. I found that she was so much more receptive to my requests —even under tight deadlines—when I made a personal connection and she saw that I truly cared about her life outside of work.

Nice Is Your Capital

This was a huge turning point for me. Seeing how well my instincts to be nice served me with Jane inspired me to embrace this intrinsic part of my personality at work. But I also didn't ignore my mentor's feedback to toughen up. I definitely needed to balance my natural niceness with a good dose of strength. Over time, I was surprised to find that owning my niceness actually made it easier for me to speak up, push back, and voice my opinions at work because I wasn't so consumed by trying to be something I was not. Instead, my confidence soared along with my effectiveness because I was finally free to be my authentically nice and caring self.

This doesn't mean it was an overnight fix. Quite the opposite, actually! It's been a lifelong struggle for me to find that perfect balance between being nice and being strong at work. But what

I learned from my experience with Jane was that I didn't have to hide that part of me any longer.

I'm so grateful that I learned that lesson when I did. Once I truly started to own my niceness, it became a huge asset throughout my career. Of course, Jane wasn't the only person who responded more positively to me when I treated her with genuine kindness and compassion. Most of the people I encountered at Ernst & Young and later at Coke; Moviefone; AOL; Time, Inc.; and then as an early stage investor and advisor were more likely to remain loyal, stick with me in a negotiation, pick up the phone, return an email, do me a simple favor, and even bend over backwards when I needed them to, all because I'd previously treated them kindly.

Yet, despite all of these experiences, I still found myself at times struggling to accept the fact that being nice was such a big part of my identity. In fact, when I was first thinking about writing this book, I had mixed feelings about it. On the one hand, I was excited about the possibility of helping other women balance kindness and strength at work, but on the other hand, I wasn't sure that being nice was what I wanted to be known for. Did it mean that people saw me as weak or ineffectual?

When I voiced these concerns to my friend and author Tiffany Dufu, she looked at me with a big, wide smile and said, "Fran, you are already known as, 'the nice person.' It's why people always call you back. It's why people will drop whatever they are doing to be helpful to you. Nice is your capital." In that moment, I knew in my heart that she was right. Being nice was a big part of my brand.

But then I started wondering—if someone like me who generally took pride in being nice had mixed feelings about this, how many other women were repressing their authentically kind selves at work because of anxiety about being perceived as a pushover? My own reaction told me that this was indeed an important subject for me to explore further.

Of course, I'm not the only woman whose niceness is her capital at work. When I asked more than 1,500 working women whether or not being nice has been helpful to them at work, 95% of them said yes. Here are some of the wonderful things these women had to say about how being nice has helped them succeed:

- "Being nice has actually been an incredible asset when I've needed to pull in favors. In my past life, I was commonly called the 'velvet hammer' because I was nice and could quickly deal with tough situations head-on. Being nice has helped me turn large teams around that were underproductive, as well."
- "Because I'm nice, I'm able to ask special favors of partners/clients when I need it; I've even stayed on good terms with nearly everyone I've laid off; my team is unbelievably loyal."
- "I feel that 'killing someone with kindness' will get you further in life than coming across as angry or mean. I am constantly told that my choice to use empathy is what makes me both a strong and approachable leader."

The Double Bind Between Nice and Strong

And yet, despite their clear understanding of how being nice has helped them succeed, these same women (76% of that 1,500, to be exact) said that they felt caught in a double bind at work between the need to be nice and the need to be tough. They reported things like:

- "I really don't like feeling that I can't be nice and assertive at the same time. It's as if I'm trying to mix oil and water even though I know it shouldn't be this hard!"
- "I'm a petite woman who looks younger than I am, so I tend to overcompensate by trying to assert my competence or stature, and I worry that it comes off wrong."

- "Women are expected to be nice, and leaders are expected to be tough. What's an ambitious young professional woman to do?"

Reading these comments, it struck me how loaded the word "nice" was for so many of these women. The majority of them believed that it was code for being weak, ineffective, a people pleaser, or a pushover. Others thought it meant someone who was pleasant to be around—a good team player, sure, but not someone who could ever stand out or be a strong leader. But I have come to learn that the strongest, most effective leaders are often also the nicest. They use their kindness to inspire their teams, encourage others, and create powerfully positive workplace environments in which their employees thrive because they're happy, engaged, and motivated.

These aren't just my observations. Research shows that a positive work environment leads to greater productivity, lower turnover, and even better health outcomes for employees, while working in an environment that is hostile, anxiety-provoking, and negative leads to lower productivity and performance—not to mention a lack of fulfillment. Specifically, happy workers were found to be 12% more productive than their unhappy peers.

This attention to environment is more important than ever in contemporary workplaces because so much of what we do every day requires collaboration rather than solo performance. A recent study from the *Harvard Business Review* found that, over the past two decades, the amount of time the average employee spends working with colleagues has gone up by over 50%. Today, we spend more than three-quarters of our workdays communicating with co-workers.

This clearly tells us that there's never been a better time for all women to reclaim our niceness and start using it to win—and to help each other win—in the workplace. The truth is that we do not have to choose between strength and kindness or confidence and likeability. We can be considerate of others *and* ourselves; accommodating *and* assertive; someone who speaks up *and* is humble; a team player who still always looks out for number one—you! And we can do that by embracing the traits of kindness and compassion that feel authentic to our personalities.

My friend Emily Dalton, the cofounder of the men's grooming line Jack Black, is a great example of this, but it took a personal tragedy for her to start owning her niceness. Emily admits that, when she was younger, she was a "goodie-two-shoes"—always seeking approval and wanting to be liked. But growing up, her professional role model was her dad, whom she describes as a "grizzly bear." He was demanding, gruff, and went into battle over anything and everything.

At the beginning of her career, Emily felt insecure about being her nice self at work, given that she had a strong role model in her rough and tough father, who was admittedly harsh, but almost always got results. She played along with this modeling, and in difficult situations, she often found herself compelled to be confrontational. This approach did get results in the short term, but it was destructive in the long term because it kept her from building stronger, more lasting relationships. Several years into her career, Emily's father grew ill and shared very honestly with her that he regretted the way he'd often acted in difficult work situations and that he, in fact, saw this as one of his personal weaknesses. Facing death, he shared the powerful insight that relationships were the only thing that really mattered.

This was a huge wake-up call for Emily. She started to transform her behavior in difficult situations, letting her natural kindness shine through. She quickly found that being nice helped inspire her team to relax, be more creative, and become less afraid to take risks. Emily saw how beneficial being nice was for her professional relationships in the long term and how often people were willing to go the extra mile for her, simply because they felt they'd been treated fairly and with respect. Emily admits she is still trying to find the perfect balance between being fair and firm, empathetic and challenging. But she is making good progress, and now, Jack Black is the number one selling prestige men's skincare brand in the United States.

Emily, along with the many successful women I'm lucky enough to call my friends (several more of whom you'll read about throughout this book), and I are proof that "nice" doesn't just help you make friends and be well liked: it can vault you to the top.

What Does It Mean to Be Nice?

First, I want you to have a clear understanding of what I'm talking about when I use the word "nice." I am not talking about someone who is merely pleasant to be around but perhaps is boring, unintelligent, or incapable of holding her own. And I'm certainly not telling you to play to the regressive stereotypes that demand constant sweetness and compliance from women.

Instead, I'm describing a woman who cares deeply about other people and who wants to connect with them, who is guided by a strong sense of values to do the right thing. She is considerate, respectful, and kind. There's a warmth and magnetism about her that draws people to her side and makes them feel good in her presence. At work, she's fair, collaborative, and generous. Instead of competing against other women, she elevates them by sharing the credit for a job well done. She has a deep, unshakable confidence that there are plenty of opportunities to go around.

My friend Patricia Karpas is the epitome of this type of woman. I met Patricia when I was working at AOL. She has held executive roles at CNBC, NBC, AOL, and Time Warner and is now a successful entrepreneur, having cofounded the award-winning Meditation Studio app. Yes, she is a total badass, and she is also one of the kindest and most grounded people I know. When I got home from the hospital after adopting my first son, Anthony, in 2010, the first thing I saw on my kitchen table was a bag of my absolute favorite cookies—the huge chocolate chip walnut ones from Levain Bakery in New York City—that she had shipped to me. I was so touched by this sweet and thoughtful gesture, and it made me think about how I've also seen Patricia use her genuine kindness to win at work.

When she was at NBC during the early days of branded television content, Patricia was tasked with working with IBM on a show they wanted to create and sponsor called *Scan* about cutting-edge technologies around the world. The problem was, the CNBC editorial team she was collaborating with didn't want an advertiser like IBM to have influence over a show's content, and IBM wanted some editorial control of the show. Because Patricia had earned the trust of both teams, she was able to make each feel comfortable enough to work together on a show that everyone was happy with. They trusted Patricia because she had taken the time to build up strong, authentic relationships with the people on both teams. This ended up being a win for Patricia, for NBC, and for IBM, and it's a great example of how Patricia intentionally used her authentic niceness to find success at work.

Another woman who I think embodies this definition of nice is Ann Moore, the first female CEO of Time, Inc. When I was working at Time, Ann was one of the most powerful women in the corporate world. She was a very strong leader. But what I really loved about Ann was that she had a very human, relational, and relatable side to her.

Every month, Ann invited people from all different departments of the company to a breakfast meeting. She started each of those meetings by going around the room and asking each of us to share something we were grateful for. It was such a beautiful way to open those meetings because it created a positive mood and helped us all see each other as three-dimensional human beings, not just someone who filled a certain role at work. Ann was always very rigorous when it came to the financial side of the business, but taking the time for things like this made working at Time, Inc. enjoyable and rewarding. Her employees tended to be loyal, which meant that her kindness was actually very good for the company's bottom line, too.

You see, it's not enough to just be nice in a general way, though that's certainly a good start. The key to making nice your super-power is to *own* your niceness and use it intentionally by connect-ing it to the things you care about. That's what Patricia and Ann have done successfully, and that's exactly what I want to help you achieve.

Don't Fake It Till You Make It

All of this is not to say that you should start putting on a phony nice façade in order to get what you want—quite the contrary! Just like my attempts to ignore my innate niceness and act tough early in my career didn't work, faking nice will never work, either. My defini-tion of nice is all about doing the right thing because it feels natu-ral to you, *not* because of what's in it for you. It's relational rather than transactional. Yes, being nice will help you get ahead, but not if you're being nice *just* to get ahead.

When you aren't being true to yourself, it's impossible to feel confident in your own skin. It's very uncomfortable to pretend to be something you're not, and it becomes nearly impossible to live up to your potential because you're so focused on keeping up the façade. True success comes when you use your talents and your genuine kindness to do work that is aligned with your values and passions. This is how you can leverage all of the best parts of you.

Without this type of genuine kindness, it's impossible to form *sustainable* relationships. Think of it this way—if your kindness is the foundation for your friendship and it's authentic, that relationship can stand strong. But if that kindness is fake, your relationship will inevitably topple.

It all goes back to trust. If you're inauthentic, people won't trust you. And without trust, there is no relationship. Research shows that our instincts tell us to ask ourselves two questions when we first meet someone: *"Can I trust this person?"* and *"Can I respect this person?"* We look to a person's genuine *warmth* and *competence* to answer these two questions.

Interestingly, the first question—*"Can I trust this person?"*— is the more important one when it comes to how we evaluate others. In fact, we only evaluate someone's competence *after* a sense of trust has already been established. This means that if someone decides they can't trust you, either because you lack warmth or display inauthentic warmth, you won't be able to get very far with them. Even worse, they'll view your attempts to come across as smart or competent as manipulative. They will resent your strength instead of respecting it.

On the other hand, according to the same study, if you come across as warm and trustworthy first and prove your competence later, people will admire your strength and evaluate you far more positively. This is a powerful argument for always leading with kindness in the workplace.

How Nice Is Too Nice?

Of course, like any other characteristic—even positive ones—it's possible to take niceness too far, both at work and beyond. If we allow ourselves to become pushovers, then our kindness stops being an asset and becomes a liability.

In fact, most of us have certain areas where we're more likely to overdo it when it comes to being nice. For example, empathy is my Achilles' heel. I have a natural tendency to worry so much about how I'm affecting others that I sometimes let that impulse get in my way. It's something I have to actively work against so that I can find balance. I share my techniques for addressing this issue throughout the book. Maybe your Achilles' heel is seeking too many outside opinions before making a decision or failing to voice your opinion on a sticky subject. Throughout the book, you'll likely become aware of certain areas where you need to embrace more kindness and other areas where you need to tone it down and start putting yourself first.

Maybe a boss or colleague has already told you that you're "too nice." A full *50%* of the women I surveyed had heard this before from bosses, colleagues, clients, and everyone in between. No wonder so many women feel caught in that double bind between being nice and being strong at work.

To me, this finding simply illustrates how important it is to reclaim "nice" and redefine it. Through your success, confidence, and all-around sense of authenticity, you can prove to those around you that being nice *and* effective are not mutually exclusive.

My friend Kat Cole has struggled with this misconception about niceness throughout her impressive career. Kat started out working at a Hooters restaurant while she was in college. By the time she was nineteen, she'd already been a waitress, bartender, and manager when the Hooters corporate office asked her to help launch the first Hooters in Australia. Kat had never even been on a plane before and was excited about the opportunity. The corporate team told Kat that one of the reasons they had chosen her for this role was that she got along so well with her peers and had been helpful to others in many different situations.

Kat was in Australia for a little over a month, and then Hooters asked her to take a leadership role in opening their first restaurant in Central America. For the next several years, Kat was promoted every eighteen to twenty-four months, in part because of her genuine kindness and generosity. She also volunteered a lot in the restaurant industry, which helped her meet mentors and build valuable relationships.

By the time Kat was twenty-six, she was one of the vice presidents of Hooters. She led all of the company's training and operational franchising and was almost always the youngest person in the room and/or the only female. Yet, amazingly, despite her extraordinary success, people constantly told Kat that she was too nice. They seemed to think that just because Kat was young and female, she needed to put on a tough-girl façade in order to get ahead.

This clearly couldn't have been further from the truth. If anything, Kat knew that she wouldn't have become so successful if it wasn't for her kindness. So when people told her that she was too nice, Kat started telling them, *"Just so we are clear, don't mistake my kindness for stupidity."*

I love this approach because it shows that Kat is not afraid to step up and own her niceness instead of apologizing for it. With that one statement, she is able to prove that her kindness does not get in the way of her strength, and indeed, Kat told me that when she says this, it often stops people in their tracks.

If people often tell you that you're too nice at work, the first step is to find out exactly what they mean. Maybe they have noticed an area where you need to exert a bit more strength, such as my need to stop yessing the Coke client to death and responding to everything with, "That's interesting." Try asking a simple follow-up question such as, "Is there a specific gap that you see?" or, "How do you think this is hurting me?" If this person does point out a specific weakness, then that's a great area to focus on as you read the rest of this book.

However, if the answer is too general, vague, or reveals that this person simply isn't accustomed to dealing with someone at work who owns her kindness, it's time to turn this assumption around. Instead of shying away from the conversation, take the opportunity to explain how you've found kindness to be an important asset at work. Maybe give the person a few examples of those times when being nice at work has helped you and the company.

Not long ago, I read an interview with Marjorie Kaplan, who led Animal Planet and TLC for years, about how she responds when people tell her that she's too nice. She said, "I've had people say to me, 'I wonder if you're too nice.' Some of that is because I'm a woman. What I have said in response is, 'I am nice. And I want to be nice. There's not such a thing as "too nice." But my expectations are high, and people do rise to my expectations. That's how I manage. I don't manage based on fear. I manage based on expectations.' It's easy for women to be read as too nice, too kind. But it's important to be able to make that choice. One of the values that I—as a person and as a woman—bring to the workplace is that I want to be nice at work. Niceness and kindness are not the opposite of ambition and drive. It is powerful to choose to be nice."

Five Ways to Respond When People Say You Are Too Nice

Try any combination of the following or come up with your own response so that you're never caught off-guard.

1. "I know, and it's really served me well!"
2. "Don't mistake my kindness for weakness."
3. "You say that as if it's something negative."
4. "I've come to realize that it is actually possible to be nice and strong. They are not mutually exclusive."
5. "It's better than the alternative . . . who wants to deal with a jerk?"

It Starts with You

Maybe until now you've been so concerned about other people's feelings at work that you've become a bit of a pushover. Or perhaps you've had a difficult time embracing your genuine kindness and have succeeded by using some rougher tactics that you don't necessarily feel great about. No matter where you currently fall on the niceness spectrum, it's okay. We're not taught how to balance being nice and strong at work, so it only makes sense that you may have veered too far in one direction or the other. Don't beat yourself up or waste time feeling guilty about it.

I see this far too often in the young women I mentor and even in more senior women in the workplace. They do the best they can at the time and then are so hard on themselves for failing to get it exactly right. Just the other day, I was talking to a company founder who is struggling with her business. She told me that, over the years, she felt the need to act tough at work in order to succeed, but now she realizes that this hard-line approach has been bad for her business in the long run. She has hurt people along the way and lost their trust, and now she feels emotionally disconnected. Even worse, she needs to raise another round of financing for her business, and she has zero support. She realized that she had made a big mistake by not being kinder to others throughout her career.

She asked me what her first step should be in making the transition to being kinder at work, and I told her that the first thing she had to do was cut herself some slack. I could hear in her voice how disappointed she was in herself, and I reminded her that she couldn't be kind to others if she wasn't first kind to herself.

So now I want to say the same thing to you. *Kindness starts with you.* If you've judged yourself harshly over the years, you need to let go of that. Remember, part of being authentically nice is embracing the real you, and you can't do that if you're busy beating yourself up for the things you've done imperfectly in the past.

It's time to stop leaving your kind and nurturing self at the door when you get to work in the morning and to start honoring your capacity for connection and relationships. Coupled with the techniques you'll learn throughout this book to be more decisive, negotiate successfully, advocate for yourself, and communicate clearly and directly in every possible workplace scenario, your authentic niceness will propel you forward on the career path of your choice. After all, nice is your superpower.

Key Takeaways

- Being nice and being strong at work are not mutually exclusive! When you own your kindness and use it with intention, it can help vault you to the top.
- When I talk about being authentically nice, I'm describing a woman who is considerate, respectful, fair, collaborative, and generous.
- Don't fake it till you make it. My definition of nice is all about doing the right thing because it feels right to you, *not* because of what's in it for you.
- If someone tells you that you're "too nice," try asking a simple follow-up question such as, "Is there a specific gap that you see?" or, "How do you think this is hurting me?"

2

Be Ambitious *and* Likeable

RIGHT AFTER I STARTED WRITING THIS BOOK, I attended the Women in the World Summit in New York City, where Hillary Clinton spoke about women leaders and likeability. Don't worry; I'm not going to get political here. Regardless of your political beliefs or what you think about Clinton, I think we can all agree that she knows a thing or two about how challenging it can be for women leaders to be seen as likeable. Sure enough, Clinton addressed the fact that for men, success and ambition tend to be correlated with likeability. That is, the more successful a man is, the more likable he becomes. But with a woman, it's the exact opposite. The more successful and ambitious a woman is, the less likeable she becomes.

There's a lot of research to back this up. In one study from Columbia University's business school, researchers described a fictional entrepreneur to a group of business students. They told one group of students that the entrepreneur's name was "Howard" and the other group that her name was "Heidi." Everything else about them was identical, but the students' responses were direct opposites. The group that heard about Howard said that he seemed like someone they'd like to work with, while the other group reported that Heidi seemed unappealing and selfish.

As I listened to Clinton talk, I felt a knot in my stomach. Everything she said rang true to me. Early in my career, women leaders were few and far between, and the ones I did encounter were often labeled as "bitchy" or "difficult" when they asserted themselves in the same way that a male leader would have been rewarded for. As a result, some of the other women I worked with went too far in the other direction. By bending over backwards to please others, they became known as being "weak" or "pushovers."

I thought to myself, *if one of the most successful and powerful women in the world still hasn't been able to figure this out, what hope do the rest of us have?* Clinton explained that, as secretary of state, she had an extremely high approval rating, but as soon as she announced her run for president, it dropped significantly. A lot has already been written about her likeability (or lack thereof), and there are certainly many other factors besides her gender that made her an unpopular candidate. But there's no doubt that this unconscious and pervasive bias against ambitious women is real.

In every industry I've worked in throughout my career, including media, finance, venture capital, and even nonprofits, women are still drastically underrepresented in leadership positions. While I had team leaders who were female at Ernst & Young, I didn't have a female boss who I reported to consistently until I was thirty-eight years old. Unfortunately, this is a cultural norm. Despite progress in the past few decades, male leaders are still more prevalent, which influences our unconscious expectations. We expect men to be ambitious, but if a woman "steps out of line," we question her motives. Why is she doing this? Why is it important to her? Is she selfish? Ultimately, we don't trust her, and that makes her unlikeable and, at times, even threatening.

As an ambitious woman who values relationships above most other things, this seemingly impossible combination is something

I've struggled with throughout my career, and it's an issue that clearly resonates with many other working women. The ones I surveyed had this to say about the fight to be seen as likeable as an ambitious woman:

- "The first word that comes to mind is 'demeaning.' The word 'nice' or 'likeable' does not sound like 'intellectual,' 'driven,' 'powerful,' 'focused,' or 'smart' (words I prefer). Instead, it's 'amenable,' a 'pushover,' 'sweet,' 'easy to get along with.' It is not what I want to identify with."
- "I think about how women are often disadvantaged because of their inclination to be pleasers, to avoid conflict, to not stand up for themselves, and to not want to seem confrontational or combative."
- "I appreciate working with women who are nice, but typically, the ones who come across as nicer seem less ambitious and aren't in leadership positions."

The issues that these women mention may sound all too familiar, but don't worry. The fact that there is an implicit bias against women who show ambition doesn't mean it's impossible to be a likeable woman leader. The way out of the labyrinth created by this double standard is *not* to focus on coming across as more likeable or less ambitious or to do anything, in fact, to try and appease stereotypes. The answer, I've learned, is to own your niceness and leverage it in a way that complements your ambition. Your authentic kindness is already inside of you. By tapping into it and using it intentionally, you'll earn people's trust, and that will allow your ambition and niceness to become equally valuable assets.

What Does It Mean to Be Ambitious?

When I think about someone who is ambitious, I think about someone who does three things: They *take credit* for their own work and ideas; they *step up* when opportunities arise; and they proactively *create opportunities* for themselves. Here are some of the techniques I use to balance kindness with each of these aspects of ambition.

Take Credit

Getting credit for your own accomplishments can be a surprisingly difficult task, especially if more aggressive colleagues are all too willing to take the credit for your work or ideas. A young woman I mentor named Reshma recently faced a frustrating situation. She was on a team that was brainstorming ideas for the name of a new product that their company was launching, and she came up with an idea that everyone in the room immediately loved. She was new at the company and was proud of herself for scoring such an important win early on.

However, her colleague John, who was running the team, went to their mutual boss and shared the new product name with him without giving Reshma any credit. In fact, she suspected that John took all the credit for the idea himself. By the time Reshma came to me, she was feeling frustrated and resentful. It was even affecting her work. She asked me why she should bother working so hard when she clearly wouldn't even get credit for her contributions.

I asked Reshma why she didn't say anything to her boss, and her response was, "I don't want to seem like I'm bragging or like I'm only doing my job to get a pat on the back. But it's still frustrating to know that someone else is getting credit for my idea." Reshma perfectly described the double bind that so many women find themselves in at work—they want to get credit for a job well done (and there's nothing wrong with that!), but they worry that taking that credit will somehow make them look bad. I suggested some ways that Reshma could take credit without feeling uncomfortably arrogant or coming across as pushy:

1) Tell a Story

People naturally love to hear stories, especially when they can learn something from that story. One way to nicely claim credit for your work is to attach a story to the win that teaches the other person something useful. For example, I asked Reshma if there was a specific brainstorming technique she used to come up with her idea. If so, she could casually share that in a manner that was more about teaching than bragging. For instance, she could mention to her boss: "When I came up with the idea for the product's name, I was using a technique called 'associative brainstorming' to free up my creativity. I'd be happy to talk to the team about this technique if you think it might help them in future sessions."

This is a much more sophisticated approach than simply asserting, "That was my idea," but the message still comes through loud and clear. Plus, it's a way of putting yourself forward as a leader who is eager to share her expertise. That's ambitious and completely non-arrogant. Bosses are always looking for people who are creative about problem solving. If you can share a strategy that applies to other problems the company might be facing, that is extremely valuable.

If your company has regular meetings in which case studies are shared about situations that have gone well and what can be learned from them, think about submitting your win as a case study. This setting gives you an opportunity to tell your story to a larger audience while also presenting a learning opportunity and, at the same time, nicely broadcasting your win.

Nominate Yourself

One way to achieve the recognition you deserve is to be included on a list of the top performers in your industry. How do you think people end up on those lists? They nominate themselves or someone at their company nominates them. Why not submit yourself to be included on an appropriate list or even for an industry award? This is a simple strategy you can use to get credit for your hard work that can potentially lead to a host of opportunities.

Some of us feel foolish doing things like this, but there's no reason to feel that way. Why not be recognized for your hard work? And if you don't win or aren't included, you haven't lost anything. If you do make a list, add it to your email auto-signature. When I see a *"Forbes* 30 Under 30" link in a founder's email, it helps them stand out in my very cluttered inbox, and they are more likely to get time on my calendar.

2) Do It One-on-One

If there wasn't a specific or teachable technique that led to the win, you can still take credit in a nice way. In these cases, I find that one-on-one interactions are more effective than group settings. It's easier to control your message and how you're being perceived in an intimate group than it is in front of a big crowd. For example, I told Reshma that when she was talking to recruiters or mentors or even colleagues, she could use those conversations as an opportunity to bring up her success in a humble way by saying, "I was really excited that the name I came up with for our company's new product was so well received."

Another option I suggested to Reshma was to let her boss know about her win by assuming that he already knew it was her idea. After all, she didn't know for sure that John hadn't shared this information with him. I encouraged her during their next weekly check-in to say something like, "Did John tell you what a great brainstorming session we had? I was so excited when I heard how much you liked my idea."

Reshma balked at this idea at first. She had a close friend in her department named Kim who had also been in the brainstorming meeting. Kim was angry on Reshma's behalf and offered to tell their boss that Reshma had come up with the idea for the name. When Reshma told me this, I was torn. On the one hand, it was a beautiful example of women supporting each other at work, and I loved that. Yet I really wanted to help Reshma summon the confidence to take credit for her own idea. I reminded her that there was nothing wrong with making it known that she was doing good work. And, by doing it without adding anything negative or accusing John of stealing her idea, she could be that perfect combination of likeable and ambitious.

3) Be Inclusive

Remember, when you have a win at work, it's pretty unlikely that you did it all by yourself, so it's important to share the credit. This sometimes causes a dilemma for "nice girls." One unfair criticism of ambitious women is that they're selfish and only out for themselves, so sharing credit when appropriate is clearly a great way to counteract this notion. But how can you avoid going too far in the opposite direction and fading into the background? Over the course of my career, I've found that it is possible to share credit without diminishing the importance of your role.

In Reshma's case, her idea didn't come at the very start of the brainstorming meeting. It was possible that someone else said something that sparked her brilliant idea, even on a subconscious level. We discussed the fact that she could share the credit by saying something like, "We were having a great conversation when that idea came to me," or, "Everyone's thoughts were so helpful in informing my idea." This felt authentic to her, and I was proud of her when she told me at our next meeting that she decided to use this approach with her boss. It clearly established her as the owner of that winning idea while also elevating the contributions of those around her.

Five Ways to Share Success with Others

- If someone who doesn't report directly to you did a good job on an important project or did something to help you earn a win, send an email to that person's boss saying so, and copy your colleague on the email. Doing so will take ten seconds and make her feel so appreciated.
- Call out a coworker's good job at a meeting. Have her stand up while everyone claps.
- Take a colleague out to lunch to celebrate teaming up on a job well done.
- Treat a colleague who helps you earn a win to a small gift card from her favorite place. For example, text her a gift certificate to Starbucks if you know she gets a latte every morning on the way to work.
- If a boss or other colleague mistakenly credits you for someone else's work, call it out without making them feel foolish. Say something like, "Wasn't that great? That was Janet's idea." Better yet, take the lead and say, "Janet came up with a terrific idea," before someone mistakenly attributes it to you.

Step Up

A huge part of being ambitious is raising your hand to jump at new opportunities. Sadly, I've seen that many of the women I've worked with and mentored over the years are less likely to truly believe in their capabilities than their male peers. There's research to support the idea of this "confidence gap." In study after study, men overestimate their abilities, while women underestimate theirs.

When Hewlett-Packard was looking to place more women in top leadership positions, they found that women were likely to apply for a promotion only when they believed they met a full 100% of the qualifications listed for the job. In other words, they only applied if they were a perfect match for the role. Men, on the other hand, felt fine applying if they met only 60% of the qualifications. This discrepancy is huge, and it directly translates into the under-representation of women in leadership positions.

I admit I've been guilty of this at times in my own career. I was working at Moviefone when AOL bought it and subsequently merged with Time Warner. I was in my early thirties and had been at Moviefone for a few years, and I was starting to feel an itch to do something different. I heard that the senior leadership was putting together a team to bridge the gap between AOL and Time, Inc. (Time Warner's magazine publishing division). There was some tension between the two divisions, so they were looking for people with particularly good interpersonal skills who could help the two groups work together.

This opportunity sounded like a great fit for me, and I loved the idea of working on the Time, Inc. brands. I wanted to step up, but I was hesitant. I had never worked in magazine publishing, and all those iconic Time, Inc. brands (*Time, Fortune, People,* etc.) were intimidating. I knew that some of the smartest people in publishing worked on those brands, and I found myself second-guessing my own qualifications.

I had a male colleague at AOL who was in a very similar situation and had the same level of experience as me. But unlike me, he jumped to make this move right away. Knowing that I had strong interpersonal skills, he encouraged me to join him. As it turned out, taking that opportunity led me to a whole new career at Time, Inc.

I now know that my colleague and I unwittingly exemplified the most common behaviors of our genders; it's typical for men to step up right away, while equally qualified women tend to hang back and wait to be pulled in. I see the women I mentor doing this all the time—doubting their own abilities and failing to step up until they feel fully and often even overqualified.

So, if women are losing ground because we undervalue our-selves, what can we do about it? The first step, simple as it may sound, is to *be aware*. If an opportunity comes your way that in-trigues you but that you think you may not be qualified for, remind yourself that you probably are a better fit than you realize.

Then, adjust your self-assessment. Remember the study show-ing that men often apply for jobs when they meet only 60% of the qualifications. So ask yourself, "Am I 60% qualified for this oppor-tunity?" If the answer is yes, go for it. A man with the exact same qualifications as you probably would. I share more techniques for building your confidence in Chapter 5.

On top of the confidence gap, women are often held back by in-advertently boxing ourselves into a narrow understanding of who we should be. Ever since elementary school, we've been taught to be "good girls" who sit at our desks all day getting work done. Studies show that elementary school teachers treat boys and girls differently, often unconsciously. They praise girls for being neat, quiet, and calm, while encouraging boys to think independently, to be active, and to speak up.

And yes, while you absolutely have to get your job done, it's also essential to keep your head *up*. By that, I mean getting up from your desk and looking at what's going on around you. Where are the opportunities and openings, the places you can wedge yourself in by volunteering to take on more responsibilities? Some of the women I've mentored avoid this because they're worried about be-ing too pushy. But I can tell you from experience how much leaders appreciate it when someone steps up to take on more responsibili-ties or seize an opportunity.

I know how tempting it can be to just stay focused, do your job, and go home, but that's not how you get ahead, and it's definitely not all that "nice girls" have to offer the world. In order to step up, you need to look up. Here are some ways to do it without feeling pushy:

1) Simplify Things

Early in my career, when I was working at Coke, I saw how much information was being thrown at my boss every day. Report after report, email after email, and meeting after meeting. Putting myself in his shoes and imagining what it was like to try and take all of this information in while managing hundreds of employees, I saw how overwhelming it must have been for him. I made it my goal to always approach him with the key information condensed as much as possible so he could quickly get up to speed and make an informed decision.

In all honesty, this created a lot more work for me. It took me hours to take a complex financial analysis that was spread across many spreadsheets and boil it down to one page with only the essential information. Of course, it would have been much easier for me to just go into his office with all of the spreadsheets. At this point, you may be thinking that this is just a story of me being subservient. But stick with me: it was actually my way of stepping up — in a nice way. I knew my boss would appreciate how I went out of my way to save his valuable time. Plus, it made it easier for my boss to make a quick decision about whatever I was presenting, and that in turn helped me be more effective in my role.

A few years later, I was only twenty-nine years old when that same boss promoted me to become the director of finance for a billion-dollar division of Coke. Suddenly, I had one hundred and forty people reporting to me, many of whom had been working at Coke for years. I didn't understand what I'd done to earn this promotion ahead of all of these people who were much more experienced and senior, not to mention older, than me. So I directly asked my boss, "Why me?"

His answer has stuck with me throughout my entire career and is something that I've shared with the hundreds of young women I've mentored over the years. He told me, "Because you're smart and you make my life easier." All those hours I had spent editing down presentations paid off. By taking on more than was asked of me, I had proven my diligence and effectiveness. I had looked up and seen what my boss really needed and then stepped up.

2) Take Something off His or Her List

Here's another thing I did for my boss at Coke that was a win for us both: observing the constant demands on his time, I offered to take initial meetings with outside vendors and other people who were looking to get on his calendar. Again, I wasn't just doing this to help him. I was stepping up and filling in the gaps that I saw as opportunities. By taking these meetings, I was able to gain valuable experience and knowledge that I wouldn't have otherwise gotten at that stage of my career. This move was also good for the company and for my boss because we were able to say yes to more meetings.

So many women in junior positions simply wait for their bosses to assign them specific jobs. And there's nothing wrong with that, but it's not exactly ambitious. Get out of your head and look at what's going on around you. Is your boss stressed and overwhelmed? If so, is there anything you can do to be helpful?

Look at what this person needs to get done and how you can contribute. Then go in and offer to step up and take on a specific task. Perhaps you can take a first stab at a report or a presentation she has to create or do some research that you know she'll need. As a boss, I was always so relieved and grateful anytime one of my team members offered to put together a first draft of a report for me. And chances are that if you participate in this way, you'll end up in the meeting where the report is being presented, gaining exposure and knowledge in the process.

This approach is so much more ambitious than merely asking, "How can I help?" Offering to help is nice, but without volunteering to take on a definite and specific task, it puts the onus on the other person. In other words, figuring out how you can help her is now just one more thing she has to do. Instead, make yourself aware of what needs doing and how you can do it. This is not just nice or a mode of serving others. It's a powerful way of stepping up and a great opportunity to gain experience working on high-profile initiatives.

Create Opportunities

If you really want to be successful, it's not enough to just step up into opportunities that are ready and waiting to be filled. Sometimes, you must create those opportunities for yourself. Taking the initiative is an important way to establish yourself as someone who is creative, ambitious, and proactive. While you're working on stepping up and into opportunities that are out there, don't forget about the endless opportunities that have yet to be identified. What can you create from scratch? These may be ideas for new customer segments, cost savings opportunities, or new technologies your company is not currently exploring.

For example, when I was at Moviefone, my colleague Cheryl Grossman and I realized that we had been so focused on selling advertising to movie studios that we were completely ignoring potential advertising revenue from other brands. I wanted to create a team that would focus on this, but I was concerned that taking the initiative would ruffle feathers. This is where being a "nice girl" came in handy. I went to my peers first—specifically, the chief revenue officer and the head of research—and got their input by asking them: "We're killing it with movie studios, but maybe we're leaving some money on the table when it comes to other brands. What are you guys seeing?"

Once I had their buy-in, I went to my boss and told him I wanted to create a small team that would focus on unlocking some advertising revenue from other brands. He gave me the go-ahead to hire two people to create this team, and we were very successful—in part because we already had the full support of my peers. When you are creating opportunities, it's essential to find the key stakeholders and bring them along with you. Make them a part of the process. By making it clear that you are looking to *collaborate instead of compete*, you'll earn their trust and their respect.

How you present the idea itself is also important. Once I became a boss, I noticed right away that my male and female employees often proceeded completely differently when they had an idea they wanted to run by me. In general, the men would pop by my office and give me a quick elevator pitch, while the women would approach me with a fully fleshed out and beautifully put-together presentation.

There's nothing wrong with being prepared; in fact, I highly recommend it. It's certainly nice to show that you've put some real thought into an idea before bringing it to your boss. But the truth is that you can create a lot more opportunities if you're not spending dozens of hours working on each one before even getting your boss's feedback. This is where you veer into people-pleasing territory.

To create an opportunity, start with a casual conversation, and then, if you receive an enthusiastic response, move on to a more formal proposal. For this initial conversation, give him or her the headline first. What is the subject you are there to discuss? Then, break your idea down into three bullet points that summarize: (1) the opportunity you are capitalizing on (or the problem you're trying to solve), (2) a few data points that demonstrate the size of the opportunity, and (3) why you're the one to address it.

Then, if you get a no, well, no harm done. You haven't invested too much into this idea, and you're free to come up with another great opportunity.

The Downside of Likeability — People Pleasing

While you work on channeling your niceness to fuel your ambitions in the workplace, remember to draw a line between being nice in a strong way and simply being a people pleaser—that is, focusing on being liked and catering to others at your own expense. Being both strong and nice is possible, but it is a delicate balance. When you veer into people-pleaser territory, it is very difficult to be seen as a strong leader instead of a pushover who's incapable of making tough decisions.

Even today, the importance of pleasing others is so ingrained in women from the time we're young girls that it's often difficult to even recognize when we're doing something to please someone else and when it's actually what we want to do. When being likeable is important to us, it's incredibly easy to tiptoe over this line before realizing that we're putting someone else's needs ahead of our own. This is something I still struggle with. So I want to take a moment here to draw your attention to the small yet essential difference between being *nice* (likeable) and being a *people pleaser*. As you go through this list, take a moment to reflect on the key differences between these two concepts.

Nice is: Positive, yet honest and straightforward
People Pleaser is: Sweeping things under the rug to avoid making waves

Research from Duke University showed that MBA graduates entering the workforce had an easier time finding jobs and higher starting salaries when they had a positive outlook and believed that their work could contribute to the company beneficially. As time went on, they were also promoted more frequently than their pessimistic peers. I certainly consider being positive an important aspect of being authentically nice, but if you're so focused on avoiding conflict that you sweep potential problems under the rug, you're not being nice—you're just being a people pleaser.

There was a time when I fell into this very trap. When I was a vice president of programming for AOL, I was working on a presentation for one of the executives. My team was tasked with presenting five ideas that would each generate over a million dollars for the company. Everyone on the team worked hard and did their part to come up with enough ideas. But then, the day before the big meeting, they shared them with me—and I was disappointed. I just didn't think their ideas were strong enough. Because my first thought was that I didn't want to cause a problem for my boss by simply asking for more time, I stayed up that whole night readying a new list of ideas to present the next day.

Unfortunately, my presentation did not go over well. In the meeting, my team members were shocked when they saw what I had done. Where were all the ideas they had worked so hard to come up with? In the end, the whole presentation fell flat, my team wasn't prepared to back me up on my ideas, and worst of all, I had done this to myself. While I had been trying to please everyone—specifically, my boss by not asking for more time and my team by not asking for more work from them—I had ended up disenfranchising and disappointing everyone in the room.

Looking back, it's so clear to me what I should have done differently. Asking the team to send me their ideas the day before the presentation wasn't nearly enough lead time to make sure we were on track. I should have had a better handle on where we were with the ideas much, much sooner.

But if I could go back and do this over again (if only!), I would tell my boss: "The ideas we have aren't as strong as they could be, and I don't want to waste your time presenting them to you. I'd rather empower the team by going back to them and giving them guidance. I'm confident that we can get there with a little more time." Far from causing problems, this tactic would have still allowed me to remain positive because it presents a solution instead of a problem, yet it's facing the problem in an honest and authentic way. That would have been the nice, effective version of what I did. Instead, I tried to please everyone and ended up pleasing no one in the process.

Nice is: Helpful

People Pleaser is: Subservient

Unfortunately, sexism is alive and well in the workplace, and women are asked to run errands, get coffee, and do favors far more often than men. Obviously, this can be demeaning and a waste of our time. Yet, part of being likeable and authentically nice is being helpful and going out of your way for others. So where do you draw the line?

This is a rule I established early in my career. I've always been happy to do favors or errands for others if (and only if) I had an authentic desire to do so or if I had a strategic reason for doing it. For example, when I was executive producer at Time, Inc. Interactive, my team was working late on a big presentation. I went to Starbucks and got them all coffee to keep them awake and motivated. When I was in more junior positions, I said yes whenever someone more senior asked for a favor. I knew that these people could be helpful to me down the road, so I was happy to help them.

But there have been many times when someone has asked me to do something, and I simply had to say no. The most egregious example of this was when I was at Moviefone. My team flew to Los Angeles for a meeting with a big movie studio. We were all sitting around the conference table when the studio executive came in. I was the only woman on my team. He went around the table and shook all of our hands, and when he came to me, he asked, "Can you please get me a cup of coffee?"

My brain went into overdrive. I wanted to say no, but I heard all the alarm bells warning me against being rude and unlikeable. At the same time, I knew that if I got him the coffee it would sabotage my authority in the meeting. That would have been a real people-pleaser move. Finally, I stood up, shook his hand, and said, "I'm Fran Hauser; I run Moviefone." He realized his error and asked his assistant to get him the coffee.

It's helpful to create guidelines so that you know what types of tasks you are going to say yes or no to. This way, you'll never get caught off guard by a request that you find yourself saying yes to and regretting later. I've seen a lot of women act passive-aggressively at work, and when I talk to them about it, I realize that it stems from resentment about all of the subservient things they've agreed to do. This is an all too common downside of being a people pleaser, and it can get in the way of your performance and success at work.

For example, when I was at AOL, I noticed that a junior designer named Jackie was rolling her eyes and making snide comments in meetings. One day, after a meeting, I asked her if she had a minute. We went into my office, and I said, "I've noticed in some meetings lately that you haven't been yourself. It seems like something is bothering you, and I want to understand what's going on to see if I can help."

Jackie was hesitant at first. "I'm not sure I feel comfortable talking to you about this," she said. I told her that she should always feel comfortable talking to me about anything that was related to her performance at work. Finally, Jackie shared that she was tired of being the "errand girl" for the entire design team. Jackie was twenty-five; this was her second job out of college, and she was a designer, not an assistant or coordinator. Yet she happened to be the most junior person on the team, so certain tasks automatically fell to her.

I asked Jackie to talk to me a little more about what she meant. As we talked through some of the responsibilities and chores she resented, I found that there were some (such as making copies for the other designers) that she'd probably have to keep doing. "I remember doing that early in my career," I told her. It seemed to help her to hear that she wasn't being singled out. Making copies was typically the most junior team member's responsibility.

But there were some tasks Jackie was doing that didn't seem

quite right. For example, every afternoon she was asked to go out and get snacks and coffee for the entire team. It was a huge disruption to her workday because she never knew when someone would ask her to go out, and then she'd have to stop whatever she was doing to collect orders from everyone before running the errand.

I suggested that Jackie talk to her manager by saying: "I'd like to get your advice on something. I love helping out the team, and I want to be a team player, but it's disrupting to go out and get snacks for everyone when I'm in the middle of designing." Framed this way, she wasn't complaining, but she was standing up for herself.

Jackie's boss responded positively and decided to create a sign-up sheet so that different team members would take turns going out to get snacks. When it was Jackie's turn, she'd know ahead of time and could control when she wanted to take a break to collect orders and go out. Jackie was able to focus more on her job, and, even better, her attitude turned around, and she became much more positive and willing to contribute in meetings.

If you're feeling unsure of whether you're being taken advantage of or if the tasks that are being asked of you are normal for your particular company's culture, ask someone at the company whom you trust for their advice. It can be a peer or a mentor or even your boss. So much of this is culture dependent. There are, of course, general standards regarding what's appropriate, but it's always helpful to talk to someone at the company who can provide additional insight.

<u>Nice is</u>: Humble
<u>People Pleaser is</u>: Putting yourself down

When you are a strong, ambitious woman, a little bit of humor and lightness goes a long way. It's endearing when any leader, male or female, doesn't take themselves too seriously. By showing a bit of humanity, it disarms those around you and makes you appear relatable and unthreatening. However, it's important not to go too far and actually put yourself down, or you risk projecting a negative self-image that could end up holding you back.

For example, when I was at AOL, I had a colleague named Marcia who was often running late. But worse, she was constantly putting herself down by saying things like, "I'm the worst," or, "I just can't get my act together." The first time I heard her say this type of thing, I thought it was funny, and it made her seem more human. After all, Marcia was a successful woman in a senior position at the company. And it's possible that she was doing this on purpose to try and make people feel more comfortable around her.

But by saying these things over and over, Marcia was undermining her own credibility. She presented herself as being so disorganized and self-conscious that people who were making decisions sometimes skipped over her and asked someone else on her team for their opinion, instead. A few times, she disagreed with the decision that had been made, which caused a great deal of conflict and dysfunction within her department.

There is a fine line between humility and self-deprecation. Pay attention to the way you talk about yourself. If it sounds harsh, critical, or demeaning, try to present yourself with a stronger dose of self-respect. You should never have to put yourself down to lift someone else up.

Likeable + Competent = Lovable Star

I'm not the only one who has noted the importance of likeability at work. *Harvard Business Review* found that, when deciding whom they'd want to work with, people value likability more highly than competence. If someone was highly unlikable, their competence became irrelevant. However, if someone was well liked but lacking in competence, their colleagues were more likely to judge them kindly and want to work with them to improve their competence. *HBR* termed the people who are both likeable and competent "lovable stars." These lovable stars have the exact combination of like-ability and ambition that so many women struggle to achieve.

Research from the University of North Carolina, Chapel Hill also confirms this conclusion. They looked at the distinction between status and likeability, particularly when it comes to teenage girls and boys, and found that the boys could have high status and likeability, while the girls who were admired were not often liked. However, when researchers followed up with teenagers ten years after high school, they found that the girls who'd been likeable (defined as caring, kind, and open) and who had used those skills in business had more positive life outcomes. Meanwhile, the high-status teen girls (AKA "mean girls") weren't doing as well ten years later. They had less successful relationships and were more likely to have problems with drugs and alcohol.

This goes hand in hand with the research you read about in Chapter 1, which found that being trustworthy was more important than being competent when it came to how someone was perceived at work. In fact, all of these studies resoundingly contradict the status quo and the conventional business world assumption that you have to be cutthroat and ruthless in order to get ahead. While niceness is commonly viewed as a weakness, my experience and this research prove its crucial importance. And when you pair your ambition with your authentic niceness, they can become the tools you need to succeed.

Key Takeaways

- There is a double standard against ambitious women: the more successful and ambitious a woman is, the less likeable she becomes. But it is possible to push back against this perception and become successful *and* well liked.
- To do this, take credit for your ideas while being inclusive, step up even when you are unsure that you are a perfect fit for a job,

and find ways to create opportunities for yourself that will benefit you and the company you work for.

- Being nice does not mean being a people pleaser! Never sweep things under the rug simply to avoid making waves, act subservient, or put yourself down. Instead, being positive, honest, helpful, and humble will make you a naturally kind and strong leader.

3

Speak Up Assertively *and* Nicely

I RECENTLY SPOKE ABOUT LEADING WITH COMPAS-
sion to a group of about one hundred university students, most of
whom were female. When my talk was over and it was time for the
question and answer session, I noticed that, out of the twenty or so
hands that went up, only one of them belonged to a female student.
Yet after I finished answering the questions and I was leaving the
stage, several female students lined up to have a chance to speak
with me one-on-one.

After the event was over, I spent some time talking to the dean
of the business school, and I pointed out what I'd noticed about the
female students who seemed more comfortable talking to me individually than asking a question in front of the entire group. He responded by saying, "The exact same thing happens at every single
event, no matter who the speaker is."

It struck me that these young women—who had so impressed
me with their confidence and intelligence in our one-on-one conversations—were still holding themselves back by not speaking
up in front of others. But it really shouldn't have surprised me.
Throughout my career, I've observed how many women have this
tendency to remain quiet at work in group situations. And, as you

read earlier, this is something that I actively had to fight against myself.

Once I did find my voice, I saw that it was necessary to speak up in order to be as effective as possible in my role. Yet, many of the women around me still fell into the trap of being seen as ineffective or weak because they never took a vocal stand. No matter how brilliant and impressive these women may have been in one-on-one discussions, not speaking up in meetings hurt their chances of succeeding professionally. When women don't share their ideas with a large number of people, their contributions are easily overlooked, and it's difficult for them to be seen as leaders. People naturally want to follow people who take a stand and voice their opinions with confidence.

Speaking up isn't just important for your own career advancement. Your thoughts, ideas, and opinions are valuable, and if they're not heard, it is truly a missed opportunity. In 2014, *Scientific American* published a groundbreaking special report on how diversity powers innovation. By studying decades of research, they concluded that groups "with a diversity of race, ethnicity, gender and sexual orientation" are more creative and innovative than homogenous groups. As a result, hearing multiple and diverse opinions consistently leads to better business outcomes. This means that no matter what industry you work in, you can help your company and your own career if you learn to speak up and add your unique and valuable perspective.

The Disease to Please

So why do so many women still subconsciously sabotage their own success by not speaking up? For one thing, women who do speak assertively are often perceived as being overly aggressive or pushy —a double standard that makes it difficult for women to know how to voice their opinions without seeming opinionated in a negative way to their peers. This goes back to a tendency to want to please others. Taking a stand will inevitably alienate someone—or so we assume—so instead we play it safe, act as people pleasers, and keep quiet.

This people-pleasing habit often begins in childhood. According to research by JoAnn Deak, Ph.D., when girls are between the ages of eight and twelve, they first become aware of how others perceive them and start "camouflaging" what they really think and feel in order to blend in better with their peers. These girls don't want to stand out, so they stop speaking up and voicing their opinions and start acting like everyone else in order to please others and fit in.

Before this kicks in, most girls have no problem expressing their own perspectives, which, if you've spent any time with a girl under the age of eight, you undoubtedly already know! But many of the tween and teenage girls Deak spoke to admitted to remaining quiet even when they had an opinion or important knowledge on a subject to avoid being seen as "too eager," "annoying," or "overbearing."

This may seem like a normal part of being a teenager, but its long-range impact can actually be very damaging. When girls begin camouflaging their true selves, just as their identities are developing, they lose out on an important chance to discover what they really think and feel and how to best express that. As a result, despite decades of women's empowerment messaging, many women in the workplace still struggle with this tendency to camouflage, hide, or dilute their thoughts and ideas rather than communicate them directly. It's one of the key issues that my mentees ask me about—how to speak both kindly and assertively—and was the number one question from the women around the country I surveyed. Here are some of the things they had to say:

- "If I keep quiet, my boss thinks I have nothing to add, but if I speak up too often, my coworkers think I'm a bitch. I just can't win."
- "I naturally communicate in a straightforward style, but this is often taken the wrong way, and people think I'm being rude. I resent feeling like I have to act like somebody else at work just to get along."
- "I have a really hard time speaking up in meetings. I usually think that other people's opinions are more valuable than mine, and I don't want to waste people's time by talking just to hear my own voice."

Does any of this sound familiar? It sure did to me. It's incredibly difficult to feel like you're constantly bumping up against an implicit bias that, as an assertive woman, you're being perceived as rude, pushy, and even angry.

Unfortunately, additional biases can make this even more complex. I recently spoke about this with Anna Chavez, the author, speaker, attorney, and former CEO of Girl Scouts of the USA. As a strong, successful woman of color, Anna felt throughout her career that she was unfairly labeled as angry or aggressive when she simply voiced her opinion at work. Yet she also had to fight to be taken seriously—an almost impossible balancing act to pull off.

Anna told me about one situation early in her career. It was the first time she had been sent out to represent a federal agency in an enforcement hearing. She was barely two years out of law school and looked young for her age. She walked into the hearing room in Aurora, Colorado, and found several men already seated at the conference table. One of the officials looked at Anna and asked her if she knew when the hearing officer would be arriving because he and his corporate colleagues were very busy and needed to get back to their office. He assumed that she was a secretary or paralegal. Anna paused and said, "Well, you're lucky. The hearing officer is here, and I am ready to start the proceedings."

All of the men were shocked that Anna would be determining the outcome of this federal hearing, and throughout the proceedings, Anna found herself trying to prove her gravitas to these men while still coming across as likeable. In the years since then, Anna has learned to stay true to herself by focusing on the good she was trying to do through her job and always trying to act as a model to others by treating them in the way she wanted to be treated. It may sound like a cliché, but this focusing inward helped her display a quiet confidence that strikes that difficult balance between strong and kind, assertive and empathetic.

To me, Anna is living proof that we don't have to give up our niceness to be powerful. We can make room for others *and* take up an appropriate amount of space for ourselves. It doesn't diminish anyone else for you to stand up straight and speak with authority. In fact, it's a gift to other women to take the space and airtime that you need because the more women stop camouflaging themselves, the more we lead the way for every woman and girl to be as powerful as they can be.

Speak Up Strategies

Back when I was struggling with all of this, my boss saw that I was having difficulty contributing in meetings and noted how very different this was from his experience of me when we met one-on-one. To urge me to speak up more, he began giving me assignments before each meeting. He would call and say, "Fran, in today's meeting, I am going to ask you to give everyone an update on the restructuring."

This gave me time to prepare my thoughts and contribute in a way that felt comfortable to me. My boss did this before a handful of meetings until I realized that I did have worthwhile things to say, with or without these assignments. And the more I spoke up, the more comfortable I felt about doing so unprompted.

If all bosses encouraged their female employees to speak up this way, I feel it would make a huge difference in the way women—and especially younger women—contribute at work. In this spirit, think about how you can help support your female peers who may be afraid to speak up. I see women sitting silently in almost every meeting I attend. One of the things I like to do is acknowledge and gently press a woman who I see is having a hard time speaking up by saying something like, "Sarah and I were discussing this earlier, and I really appreciated her perspective. Sarah, can you share your thoughts with the group?"

Yes, it does help when you've prepped this person in advance so she's ready when you turn to her instead of simply putting her on the spot. Another tactic I use is to give new team members the opportunity to enjoy a small win that will boost their confidence, and then I acknowledge the win in a group meeting. For example, "Maria just hit her target goal yesterday. Congratulations. Can you let the team know how you did that?"

While I was working on finding my voice, I relied on the following techniques to encourage myself to say more and have more of a presence in meetings:

- I prepared ahead of time by looking at the agenda and doing my homework so I knew I would have something of value to add. If there was no published agenda, I asked the meeting convener for a list of topics to expect.
- Before every meeting, I made an active commitment to myself to make at least one comment in the meeting besides a simple throwaway line like "Yes" or "That's interesting!"
- Rather than wait for an opening (I wanted to be nice and avoid

interrupting), I made an effort to speak first when a topic was opened up for comments.

- Then I started with a stock phrase to get myself started, such as:
  - "I have a suggestion . . ."
  - "I did some informal research and discovered . . ."
  - "Here's what I've been thinking . . ."
- I also came up with a few phrases that helped me jump into the middle of a conversation:
  - "I really like that perspective, and . . ."
  - "That reminds me of . . ."
  - "Following on that, I wonder if we . . ."

Another technique I started using, almost subconsciously, was to actually repeat half of another person's sentence and then build onto that thought. At first, this was simply a way for me to feel comfortable speaking up, but my colleagues have repeatedly told me that it helps them feel more confident in their own opinions. Anything that helps both parties feel more positively about how they're communicating is definitely a win-win.

Speech Weakeners and Strengtheners

When you do speak up, make sure to do so from a position of authority and strength. As you read earlier, women sometimes camouflage their thoughts and opinions in many unconscious ways that dilute their effectiveness.

There are specific habits and phrases that either strengthen or weaken our speech. Very often, we do these subconsciously, perhaps as a result of the camouflaging we started back in grade school. If you're not sure whether you are guilty of any of these, ask a trusted colleague to pay attention to what you say and how you say it in a meeting and give you honest feedback. Then, commit to eliminating the habits that dampen your effectiveness.

"Sorry, Not Sorry"

One thing that women do too often to avoid coming across as bitchy or rude is apologize—even when we have done nothing wrong. You are probably already familiar with this phenomenon. Have you ever found yourself apologizing when someone else bumps into *you*? Or have you ever gotten the wrong meal at a restaurant and apologized profusely to the waiter for sending it back? The journal *Psychological Science* published a study that showed women do indeed apologize more frequently than men. Unfortunately, when we do this at work, it can cause us to seem like pushovers.

When I realized that I was apologizing too much at work, I became determined to break this habit. I started by searching my sent emails for all mentions of the word "sorry" to get a better sense of when, how, and to whom I had been apologizing without realizing it. I soon found that I'd apologized for all sorts of things, like waiting more than a day to respond to an email ("Hi John, I'm sorry it's taken me so long to respond . . .") or that I wasn't available to meet at the time a colleague suggested ("I'm so sorry, I won't be available then, but how about . . .").

Reading these emails, it was so clear to me that I had accidentally been putting myself in a weak position by apologizing for these trivial things. Why was I implying that I was responsible for responding to the email immediately or that I was expected to work around the other person's schedule? Without realizing it, I had been making myself seem subservient. From that point on, I started rereading all of my emails before sending them specifically to make sure they didn't include unnecessary apologies. I also downloaded the brilliant "Just Not Sorry" Gmail plug-in, a Google Chrome extension that highlights phrases in your emails that may be undermining the real message you want to send.

It was also helpful for me to replace my automatic "sorry" with something else. When I sat down and thought about what I was actually trying to convey with the word "sorry," I realized that what I really wanted to communicate was my gratitude and appreciation for the other person's time. So I started replacing "I'm sorry" with "Thank you." It's a simple tweak, but this dynamic truly changes everything. Saying "Thank you" is much stronger than "I'm sorry" and is much more aligned with what I was really trying to express in the first place.

If you have a tendency to overuse the word "sorry," think about what you're really trying to say. Try to find another word or phrase that's stronger and closer to your true intent. Remember, there's never a need to apologize if you haven't done anything wrong.

But "sorry" isn't the only word that can weaken a nice woman's speech. Nicole Williams, author of the book *Girl on Top*, identified the following speech weakeners that women often use in our attempts to be accommodating. Start paying attention to whether or not you do any of these. For the first two, you can read over your emails to make sure you're not including them. For the others, try to find a coworker who can act as an "accountability buddy" and give you a signal every time you apologize unnecessarily or accidentally weaken your speech. The more aware you become of this, the easier it will be for you to speak up confidently and clearly.

Common Speech Weakeners:

- Voicing an opinion by saying, "I might be wrong about this, but . . ." By starting your sentence this way, you are discrediting your own idea before you even say it.
- Failing to take ownership of your idea by saying "I feel" instead of "I know."
- Making an assertion into a question by raising your voice at the end of your sentence. This phenomenon, also known as "upspeak," is one of the main ways that women make themselves seem passive instead of strong and proactive.

- Shrugging or looking down when speaking. This kind of body language makes us seem less confident and capable.
- Communicating a lack of commitment to our statements by allowing our voice to trail off at the end of our sentence.

Of course, one of the main reasons women end up using the above speech weakeners in the first place is that we're afraid that if we voice a strong opinion, we'll be perceived as being overly aggressive. But the truth is that you don't have to choose between staying quiet and sounding harsh. You can express yourself clearly and strongly and still be perceived as the authentically kind person that you are.

To find the right balance, let's take a look at a situation that requires speaking up and examine three options for how to do it most effectively. Let's say you're in a team meeting discussing a situation where a definitive recommendation needs to be made. There is a lot of discussion back and forth and a lot of swirl, but no one is taking a stand. You feel that you have a good idea on how to proceed. Here are three ways in which you can choose to speak up:

1. Too weak—"I'm not sure how everyone else will feel about this, but I think . . ." This displays that you're not confident in your recommendation and relies too much on feelings rather than facts.
2. Too abrupt—"I've figured it out; here is what we are doing." This centers only on you as a person and doesn't give credit to anyone else who contributed during the brainstorming session.
3. Just right—"Hearing everyone's thoughts has been really clarifying for me; here is what I think we should do to move forward." This is a good balance between acknowledging others' input and confidently voicing your opinion. Like Goldilocks said, this one is just right. Remember, striking this balance is going to take

practice; the important thing is that you commit to making your voice heard, and the words will get easier over time.

Disagreeing Nicely

Speaking up and voicing your own opinions means you'll inevitably disagree with other people from time to time. How can you do this without feeling like you're picking a fight or alienating the other person?

This tension is something that made speaking up difficult for me when I first began my career. The very concept of disagreeing vocally was not aligned with my background as someone who was always taught to be polite and respectful. It just never occurred to me to express my own contradictory opinions. It was rude to disagree in public, right? So when I disagreed with something that came up at work, I remained silent—*especially* if the person I disagreed with was senior to me.

I first began pushing back when my boss encouraged me to do so at Ernst & Young, but I didn't fully make the adjustment until I was at Coke and my boss there said, "I expect people to debate me, question me, and disagree openly because I believe this is the way to build the best products and businesses."

This concept was so foreign to me. But that's what he was asking for, and of course I wanted to deliver, so I had to actively and consciously change my perspective. I started debating with him openly. In truth, this didn't feel right to me, either, but over time, I learned that I could voice a contrary opinion with a sense of empathy by making an effort to see the situation from the other person's perspective.

I found that if you think about whom you're talking to *and* what he or she cares about, it's much easier to express your point of view without accidentally rubbing the other person the wrong way. This gives you the best chance of being heard, even when you're expressing a contrarian point of view. This approach helped me substantially with presenting my views. It also helped me find the balance between being nice and assertive. Here are my tips:

Rely on the Power of Questioning

When I disagree with someone, my first step is to ask a lot of questions to try and understand the critical junctures in the other person's thought process. When you learn more about where someone you disagree with is coming from, you may find yourself coming around to their position. Alternatively, they may observe on their own that there is a flaw in their logic or decision-making process.

Even if you still disagree after hearing their answers, asking questions is an important aspect of communicating, especially when you disagree with someone. It shows that you are being thoughtful and will hopefully illuminate the other person's thinking. Posing questions has also often helped me stand firmer in my own convictions. These are a few questions I rely on in a disagreement:

- "Can you tell me about how you came to that conclusion?"
- "What source did you use for that data point?"
- "What led you to that assumption?"

Get an Outside Perspective

One approach that I recommend is talking to other people who have a deep understanding of what the person I'm trying to communicate with is thinking. I recall when a woman I mentored named Layla started a new job as the director of marketing at a company that created event management software. After a few weeks on the job, she found that she and her colleague Carlos, who was the director of sales, did not see eye-to-eye about where the marketing department's responsibilities ended and the sales team's job began. Layla knew she had to have a direct conversation with Carlos about this, or else she'd feel like she was being a pushover. But she was dreading the conversation and didn't want to ruffle feathers so early in her tenure at the company.

I suggested that, before talking to Carlos, Layla go to one or two people who worked closely with him to probe more deeply into his perspective by finding out more about the company's history. This wasn't about going behind Carlos's back, but instead gaining a deeper understanding of the overall context so that Layla could fully appreciate where Carlos was coming from.

You may be wondering why I didn't suggest that she just go and ask Carlos himself. Well, first of all, Layla already knew what Carlos thought. What she didn't know was *why*. Sometimes it's hard for people to be objective about what forms their own opinions. By talking to people who worked closely with Carlos, Layla received valuable insight into his thought process that was both accurate and objective. She also developed a sense of context, which is essential when preparing a counterargument.

It's easy to walk into a new situation with your guns blazing and start making immediate changes. And sometimes organizations do need a fresh eye to see where things can be improved. But it's also important to respect a company's history and culture. The people who've been there longer than you and are invested in the company's ways are likely to take real offense to any drastic changes. You can use your authentic niceness to push through necessary changes by first educating yourself about how the company has handled business in the past and, more importantly, why.

For example, I told Layla to find out why the marketing and sales departments were set up the way they were by asking the CEO to explain how those departments had evolved since the company's inception. She learned that back when Carlos had first started at the company, it was so small that he was in charge of both sales and marketing. When the company grew and they hired a marketing person, Carlos handed over the responsibilities that he enjoyed the least and continued doing everything else himself.

From Layla's perspective, the team divisions were inefficient, and while that was certainly a valid observation, she needed to keep in mind that Carlos had created these departments from the ground up and was fully committed to keeping things the way they were. I told Layla that she had the right to stand up and suggest some changes, but acknowledging the company's history would help her do so in a kind and empathetic way that wouldn't shock or offend Carlos.

Start from Their Side

When it was finally time to have the key conversation, I suggested that Layla start by making it clear that she had taken the time to see the company from Carlos's perspective. She could say, "Here's my understanding of where you're coming from. And by all means, please correct me if I'm wrong." This respectfully showed Carlos that she cared about his perspective before she shared her own.

Once he saw that Layla had empathy for his point of view and wasn't going to jam any major changes down his throat, Carlos was able to relax a bit, and Layla continued, "I understand why you originally set up these departments the way you did, and I'm so impressed with how you handled all of that on your own for so long. Now that I'm on the team, I can take some of those responsibilities off your plate. Can we discuss making some structural changes?" Layla put Carlos at ease, and this put her in a great position to actually be heard by him and then implement the changes that she thought would be best for the company.

Five Nice Ways to Segue into a Disagreement

After I've gained an understanding of the other person's perspective, the context, and the history, here are the phrases I use to actually voice my contrary opinion:

- "I completely respect where you are coming from on this, and . . ."
- "That's a valid point, and . . ." (It's much less abrasive to say "and" instead of "but.")
- "Let's explore this together; tell me a little more about . . ."
- "It sounds to me like we both want . . ."
- "Let me share with you . . ." (This is much more collaborative than "Let me tell you . . .")

Speaking Up to Impropriety

Like most women, I've faced a handful of occasions throughout my career when men have made sexist or rude comments to me. These situations are always difficult, and it can be incredibly challenging to speak up in a way that feels authentic when you're caught off-guard by a remark that makes you feel deeply uncomfortable.

When I was in my early thirties, I was in a meeting with a senior executive at my company. We were gathered in a conference room, working late one night to meet a big deadline. The general discussion centered on a few new features that would be included in a website redesign. Specifically, we were talking about what size the main photo on the home page should be. The conversation turned to the types of photos that we could post to get the highest response.

Out of nowhere, the senior executive said, "Let's post a photo of Fran in that short dress she was wearing the other day. That would get a lot of clicks." The room went totally quiet. It was beyond awkward. I froze for a second and then said, "Can I please talk to you outside?"

We went out into the hallway and I told him flatly, "If you want to get the best work out of me, that is not the way to do it." I could tell by the look on his face that he was horrified, and he apologized immediately. He explained that it was late, and he was just trying to lighten the stress in the room, given the deadline. There may have been some truth to that, but it really didn't matter. I told him that, whatever his original intention was, saying something like that was completely unacceptable.

He apologized profusely, and what he did next really surprised me. When we went back into the room, he apologized to the whole team. He said that he was trying to lighten the mood, but that what he had said was completely inappropriate and that he had so much respect for me and for the work that I do.

This was a really important moment for me in terms of setting an example for the other women in that room. At that moment, I was so tired and drained from working so late that I didn't overthink my response ahead of time. And the response that had popped out actually ended up serving me well. When I thought about it later, I saw that he might not have responded as positively if I had called him out on it in front of everyone. I didn't need to do that. Everyone immediately knew that I was standing up for myself when I asked to talk to him outside. Tying my response to my performance was also key because it allowed me to remain objective while talking about such an awkward and personal subject.

Offhand and unwanted comments like this do happen, but I have to say that I never heard any inappropriate comments from that particular executive again. If I had, then I would have definitely approached HR about it. If you face a situation like this, there is nothing wrong with going to HR right away, but I found it very effective to call it out in the moment, in private, and in a way that was directly tied to my performance.

My dear friend Adaora Udoji, a media executive, producer, and investor, shared a story with me about a time early in her career when she had to speak up for herself. She was still in law school when she went for an interview with a deputy chief counsel. As soon as Adaora walked in the door, the man who was going to interview her took one look at her, a young woman of color, and said, "You don't look anything like a tax lawyer."

Adaora's heart sank. She really wanted this job and had done so much work to prepare. This seemed so unfair. But what could she do? She knew that she had the right qualifications for the job, but how could she respond in a way that would convey that his comment was out of line without alienating him entirely? After pausing for a moment, she said calmly, "I think tax lawyers come in all shapes and colors."

From there, Adaora tried to engage herself fully in the substance of their conversation. The man she was interviewing with soon saw that she knew her stuff, and she ended up feeling good about their conversation, even though she didn't get the job. Adaora told me that the experience was painful. It hurt her, but it didn't end her. In fact, it left her feeling hopeful that he wouldn't make the same assumptions the next time a woman of color walked in the room. I was so inspired by Adaora's approach and her desire to increase opportunities for the other women who will come up behind her. I hope that if something like this happens to you, you'll find the courage to speak up and encourage the other women at your company to do the same.

The "Nice Girl" vs. the Bully

The first time I had to deal firsthand with a bully at work was when I was in my early thirties, shortly after AOL acquired Moviefone. We were based in New York City, and my boss asked me to partner on a project with Ryan, who was based on the West Coast. It didn't take me long to see that Ryan was toxic. He was mean, he yelled, he interrupted me in meetings constantly, and he micromanaged like crazy. To make things even worse, he was completely ineffective. He frequently made big promises—like being able to connect with an A-list actor to be part of a program we were working on—and then he never followed through.

My strategy in working with Ryan was to simply focus on getting the work done. While relationships with colleagues have always been important to me, I knew that engaging with Ryan on a personal level would not be productive. So I did my best to stay true to myself while still keeping my distance and tuning out his negativity.

Unfortunately, this approach only worked for so long. The final straw came when he called me at home on a Sunday and yelled at me about the A-list actor not being on board (even though this part of the program was his only responsibility). For what felt like ten minutes, he would not let me get a word in as he ranted about how I'd failed.

Finally, he stopped to take a breath, and I jumped at the chance to respond. I told him very directly, "Ryan, I'm confused. I thought it was your responsibility to secure the celebrity. But regardless, at this point the program will be fine without him, and we're wasting energy discussing it because it's too late; we launch in two days." He started yelling again, and I said, "I'm not going to listen while you speak to me this way." I hung up and decided in that moment that I would no longer work with him.

The next morning, I went to my boss and explained the situation. I made sure to use only the facts of what had happened—not just the day before, but also in previous instances—and not base the conversation on feelings. Finally, I said, "I have given it my best try, and I can no longer work with Ryan. I think it would be best if you take him off the program. He is not only a bully, but he's also ineffective."

My boss tried to convince me to give it another shot. "I can't do that," I said. "His behavior is abusive. I won't tolerate it, and I don't want my team to be exposed to it." I was very calm yet firm in my delivery, and I was glad that I'd taken time to calm down after the conversation the day before. My boss ultimately agreed, and Ryan was taken off the program.

I've thought a lot about this experience with Ryan in the years since then, and I've also seen bullying take on many different forms at work—not just yelling or hurling insults, but also talking behind someone's back, sabotaging their work, or spreading negative rumors. These are extremely difficult situations, and they can be even more challenging for "nice girls" who so value getting along with their coworkers and are often very likely to take a bully's actions personally.

Throughout the years, I have learned to recognize that someone else's bad behavior has nothing to do with me and then separate myself from it by acknowledging that I am powerless to change it. All I can do is act with intention. When I've faced situations like this, I've found it useful to choose one or more of the following three courses of action:

Set Emotional Boundaries

If you acknowledge to yourself that this person is a bully and are determined not to let it bother you, by all means, try and make it work. But if you do this, make sure you have people in your corner who will support you and protect yourself by setting emotional boundaries. Do not engage in drama, and never allow yourself to get swept up in someone else's bad behavior. It takes a lot of confidence and self-knowledge to stay true to yourself in this type of environment. Often, we "nice girls" carry around a tiny seed of doubt that a conflict is somehow *our* fault. When a bully spots that doubt, he or she will be very likely to prey on it.

If you find yourself in a situation like this, look for allies at work who can remind you that this behavior has nothing to do with you. Then, when you see it take place, simply acknowledge it—"Oh, it's happening again"—and remind yourself that he or she is the one with the problem, *not you*. This is a simple but powerful way of separating yourself from the other person's toxicity.

My friend Jack once faced a situation like this at work. He had a client who was consistently insulting and abusive despite Jack's many efforts to make the relationship work. Jack prides himself on developing strong relationships with his clients, so to some extent he couldn't help but blame himself. But when he finally went to the client's boss and explained, "I can't seem to make this relationship work; I'm afraid I'm not the right fit," the boss responded by saying, "Five other people have come forward with the same types of issues. It's not you."

This truth is so important to remember, especially if you're a "nice girl" who prides herself on getting along with everyone. *It's not you.*

Call It Out

This is what I did with Ryan, and it's a strong option if you are in good standing at your company and have supporters who will stand up for you. Calling out a bully takes a lot of guts, but it's often worth it. Not only do you stand a good chance of forcing this person to improve his or her behavior, but you are also taking a step toward creating a kinder and healthier work environment.

It's important to note that I did not report Ryan's behavior the first time he said something disparaging to me. Good people make mistakes, and this doesn't automatically mean that they are bullies. If someone makes one inappropriate comment (like the executive who commented about posting a picture of me in my skirt), I recommend addressing it directly and then moving on. But if the behavior is consistent, it's time to question whether it constitutes bullying.

There is often a fine line between a person who isn't as nice as you'd like and someone who is actually abusive. Some people aren't interested in developing relationships at work and are completely focused on getting the job done, so they act demanding and cold instead of warm and fuzzy. That's not ideal, but it's not abusive, either. To me, the definition of a bully is someone who makes consistent personal attacks or comments that are degrading, demeaning, insulting, offensive, or sexually inappropriate.

If you are indeed being bullied, gather as much evidence as possible (emails, etc.), and then go to HR or to the other person's boss if you have a good relationship with him or her and calmly explain the situation. To make sure it comes across as a professional conversation rather than tattling, focus on facts and how this person's behavior is affecting your work rather than how it makes you feel. I also recommend starting this conversation the same way as any difficult discussion—by directly saying, "This is going to be a difficult conversation," or, "This is something I've been really struggling with."

Move On

The unfortunate truth is that there are a lot of bullies who are deeply entrenched in a workplace environment and aren't going anywhere. Sometimes it's even your boss who is the bully. If you've gone to HR and the situation has not improved or you sense that the bully is well protected and has a lot of political power within the company, it may be best to start looking for another job. Ultimately, you have to weigh the pros and cons for yourself based on how much exposure you have to this person and how much it is affecting you and your work.

This is one reason you should focus on networking (see Chapter 7), so that you never find yourself stuck in a bad situation with nowhere else to turn. When you make networking a priority, you develop a large safety net comprised of individuals who can help you find a position in a healthier environment. Create this net before you need it!

If you do leave your job for this reason, I recommend being

candid during your exit interview with HR. Tell them, "One reason I was open to other opportunities is that this wasn't an entirely healthy work environment." Hopefully, the company will not want to lose any more talent and will finally take care of this problem.

> **Here are a few phrases that I rely on when I'm dealing with a bully:**
>
> - "Please don't talk to me that way."
> - "Let's try to get this conversation to a place where it can be productive."
> - "Let's take a break and come back to this later."

Woman Spreading: Improving Your Nonverbal Communication

It's not just what we say, but *how* we say it that telegraphs our strength or weakness to others. Albert Mehrabian, a psychology professor at UCLA, is a pioneer in the study of communication. He theorizes that your credibility is judged 58% by your overall body language, 35% by your tone of voice, and only 7% by what you actually say. Pretty shocking, isn't it? Once I learned this, it served as a kind of wake-up call. I really started to focus not just on the content of my communication, but also on how I said it and what body language I used when I spoke.

This requires taking an honest look at yourself and deciding what you can improve. Do you slouch, avoid eye contact, or speak too softly? Many of us have as much trouble with body language and our tone of voice as we do with speaking up, which takes us back to the old issue of "camouflage." Many women have unconsciously trained themselves from girlhood *not* to stand out from the crowd. This includes how we speak, stand, sit, and even how much space we take up.

Recently there has been a lot said in the media about the fact that men take up much more physical space than women do, irrespective of size. Men do it unconsciously, claiming power and asserting dominance in every room they enter, while women tend to diminish their presence, often due to the messages we received in early childhood to shrink ourselves in order to make space for others.

This is, unfortunately, something that society reinforces in girls and young women. "To this day," writes feminist author Soraya L. Chemaly on the website *Role Reboot*, "when I sit—in a chair, on a bus, a train, at a desk—I hear my primary school headmistress explain that ladies never cross their legs at the knees. The thought of sitting, arms stretched out on either side on the top lip of the back of, say, a park bench is laughable to me, it's so physically alien. Usually, in public space, I fold myself up and try, by habit, to make room for others. [Unconsciously, in our early childhood training] we are saying to our girl children, empty yourself, lack substance, embody frailty . . . *Be as small as possible* and we will love you more. To our boy children we say, take up *more room*, more than is good for you or that you need. Be as big as possible."

There's some interesting new research from the Stanford University Graduate School of Business that shows how women leaders can use body language to come across as powerful at work without seeming overly dominant or aggressive. Because nonverbal behaviors work on a mostly subconscious level, people view a woman who uses strong and powerful body language at work less harshly than a woman who *speaks* in a strong and powerful way.

My friend Jane Hanson, who was a news anchor for many years and is a communications expert, refers to this as "woman spreading." Knowing that women are viewed as natural leaders when they take up more space, she encourages women to stand tall, uncross their legs, and drape their arms over their colleagues' chairs.

Don't hesitate to take up more physical space at work. People will view you as a natural leader if you display physical confidence. This may feel completely foreign to you if you're used to camouflaging your body language, but with a little practice, it will start to come more naturally.

Not long ago, I was at a board meeting during which one of my fellow board members (a man with a naturally strong voice) was being very talkative and had a lot of opinions. My voice was not as loud, and the only way I could get a word in edgewise would be by shouting, which I was not going to do. So I decided to stand up, walk around behind my chair, and then speak. This worked like a charm. He stopped talking and listened intently to what I said. When Jane told me about "woman spreading," I realized that's exactly what I had been doing, and it had worked.

"Nice Girl," Interrupted

Chances are that if you're a woman, you're very familiar with how it feels to be interrupted when you're speaking at work. This can be infuriating and demoralizing, and it's happened to me more times than I can count. In a 2017 article, the *New York Times* stated that "being interrupted, talked over, shut down or penalized for speaking out is nearly a universal experience for women when they are outnumbered by men."

I'm sure this isn't news to you, so the question is, what can you do about it? I have found that focusing on my nonverbal communication has helped cut down on how often I'm interrupted at work. When I sit up straight or even stand up and force myself to take up a lot of space, make eye contact with whomever I'm speaking to, lean in, and remain extremely engaged, I find that I am less likely to be cut off or interrupted. But, of course, this does still happen to me from time to time. When it does, I kindly but firmly say, "Excuse me, I wasn't finished."

Don't let yourself be interrupted. Take up space so that the people around you are forced to respect your presence. And if it still happens, have a line like this that you've rehearsed ahead of time so that you're always ready to speak up against being spoken over.

Key Takeaways

- Failing to speak up in meetings can and will hold you back at work. Make a pact with yourself to voice a thought or opinion in every meeting you attend.
- Look out for speech weakeners. Reread your sent emails to make sure you don't say "sorry" for no reason or otherwise weaken your communication.
- When you disagree with a colleague, use your natural empathy to try and see the issue from their perspective before directly and clearly voicing your opinion.
- Remember, nonverbal communication is extremely important. Be cognizant of your posture, eye contact, and the amount of physical space you take up.
- Keep an eye out for other women who are sitting quietly in meetings and nicely encourage them to speak up, too.

4

Give Feedback Directly
and Kindly

WHEN I WAS TWENTY-SEVEN, I TOOK ON MY first real managerial role as corporate controller at Coke. As a new manager, some aspects of the job came more naturally to me than others. One aspect I felt comfortable with right away was serving as a mentor and coach to my team members, and I fully embraced this part of the job. I made sure my team knew that they could come to me with challenges, and I'd act as a sounding board and supporter.

Because of this, my team members saw that I truly cared about them and their careers, and knowing that they were happy in their roles made me feel good as their boss. It was all sunshine and rainbows until the first time I had to take on another new managerial responsibility — giving negative feedback.

This was a huge shift for me, and I struggled with the idea of having to give tough feedback for a few reasons. First and foremost, as someone who deeply values kindness, I had a lot of empathy for my team members. I knew how hard it would be for them to hear critiques, and when I put myself in their shoes, I couldn't bear the thought of making them feel that way. Second, taking a negative tone just didn't come naturally to me. I was so much better at being the good cop, and acting tough felt wrong, like I was playing a role.

At the same time, I knew that I couldn't be the good cop all the time, or I'd fall into the trap of being seen as a pushover. I was, frankly, stumped and worried that I would be seen as overly harsh or too mean if I gave my team straightforward feedback.

With all these conflicting factors piling up around giving honest feedback, I did what any "nice girl" would do—I completely avoided it! The story you read in Chapter 2 about me staying up all night to redo the presentation when my team members' contributions fell short is the perfect example of this. I just couldn't bring myself to give them feedback in a clear and straightforward way, and we all remember how that backfired on me.

Soon enough, though, I had to find a way. Kira, a financial analyst on my team, was proving to be a weak link. She was very effective at financial reporting—I could count on her for accurate spreadsheets, charts, and tables that communicated the financial position of the company. That part was great. There were two problems, however. First, Kira never delivered her reports on time, and second, the accompanying write-up explaining the financial results was usually poorly written, full of grammatical errors, and failed to clearly communicate the financial picture the way I needed it to.

For months, I had avoided giving Kira direct feedback. Instead, I rewrote all of her copy, and when Kira inevitably sent me the numbers at the very last minute, I pulled all-nighters to get the cleaned-up reports to my boss on time. Yet, I knew this approach was not sustainable. If I continued to say nothing, the next quarter would be the same, and the one after that, and the one after that. Even worse, if my team knew they could hand in sloppy work and I'd simply redo it, I'd be undermining my own authority as their boss. I'd be the walking definition of a people pleaser! I couldn't let that happen. I needed to give Kira real, constructive feedback, but I didn't know how to do it in a kind way that felt authentic to me.

I went to my boss and explained the bind I felt I was in. He told me that I was actually doing Kira a disservice by cleaning up her work rather than being direct with her about her performance. He urged me to address the issue head-on. He also suggested that maybe the reason Kira was consistently late in submitting her reports was because she was getting stuck on the writing. He recommended that I start my conversation with Kira by addressing the missed deadlines and see if the writing challenges came up naturally.

Emboldened by this advice, I thought back to the feedback I'd gotten from bosses throughout my own career and how their different approaches had made me feel. Two different experiences stood out to me right away, both with team leads at Ernst & Young. One of them launched immediately into negative feedback during my performance review in a way that was really startling and hard to process. Yet, she did a good job of clearly communicating what needed to change and pointing to specific examples. I left that meeting feeling a bit deflated, but knowing exactly what I needed to do to improve.

The other team lead, however, started my performance review by telling me how much she valued me. She asked me questions and didn't rush through the meeting. This conversation felt like much more of a dialogue. Yet, I left feeling as though she hadn't really pinpointed any areas for potential growth. The conversation was more pleasant, but it wasn't nearly as constructive.

As I thought about this, it struck me that I could combine these two approaches—the directness of my first team lead with the kindness of the second. If I gave Kira feedback that was nice *and* direct, it would feel natural to me and hopefully help Kira improve her performance without crushing her spirit. It was a matter of giving her feedback in an empathetic and supportive way by presenting it as helpful advice rather than as a harsh critique. This new mindset allowed me to give feedback while drawing on the skills like empathy and compassion that felt authentic to me.

Newly confident in my approach, it was so much easier for me to have that formerly daunting conversation with Kira. I began our conversation with the positive, which was that she was doing a great job on the numbers. It was easy to praise her on this because it was true. Then I moved on to the missed deadlines. I told her that I wanted to be helpful to her and that I wanted to understand what was driving the late behavior, but I also wanted her to know that her missing deadlines was creating a burden for the team.

As soon as I brought it up, amazingly, Kira seemed relieved. My kindly worded feedback gave her an opening to admit that she did not enjoy the writing part of the report. She told me that, while she always had the numbers prepared well in advance, she struggled to get through the commentary. We spoke about whether her writing was something that she wanted to work on improving or if she wanted to transition to a quantitative-only role, where she could create the most value for the company and for herself.

The conversation ended up being a huge relief for both Kira and for me. And it completely changed the way I thought about providing tough feedback. I now see feedback as almost a kind of gift to the other person. It's also a gift to myself as a manager. If I hadn't spoken to Kira when I did, I probably would have spent months redoing her work and holding it against her. It was much better for both of us to have that conversation. Most important, by learning that even negative feedback can be approached with a real sense of empathy, I was able to leverage my authentic kindness in a way that was productive for my team and for me.

Stephanie Kaplan Lewis, the cofounder of Her Campus Media, recently shared a story with me about her kind approach to giving negative feedback. She had to give a very tough performance review to an employee whom she liked a lot and was quite close with, but who just wasn't performing. Stephanie made sure to cite specific examples to illustrate the critiques she was making so that the critiques didn't feel too personal or unsubstantiated. She also made sure to mention those elements of the job this person had done well and the strengths she saw in her. While the review was a tough one, the message throughout was that Stephanie was confident in her employee's ability to improve and had every intention of working with her to make sure her next review was nothing like this one.

The employee responded incredibly well and left the review motivated to make changes. Only four months later, she had made enormous improvements and was on track to get a promotion, rather than "checking out" after a bad review. Stories like this motivate me to continue striving to balance my kindness and directness whenever I have to give the gift of constructive and specific feedback.

Your Brain on Feedback

If you're not yet in a managerial role or can't even imagine a time when you will be, it's still important to think about how to communicate feedback. It speaks to the larger struggle that many women face when trying to balance being nice and strong at work. As you can imagine, I'm not the only woman who's ever had a hard time giving constructive feedback. Yet, it's something we must learn to do. As Dawn Casale, the founder of One Girl Cookies, says, "If I have to have a difficult conversation and don't have it, I'm sending the message, 'feel free to take advantage of me.'"

Here are some of the responses the women I surveyed had to say about the issue of negative feedback:

- "I constantly find myself editing what I want to say to make sure I'm not coming across as mean or critical when I'm just trying to help my team perform better. It really bothers me that this is something male bosses don't seem to have to worry about."

- "If I don't give tough feedback, I worry that I'll be seen as a pushover, so I always go out of my way to deliver the news like my male bosses would—with no emotion or sugarcoating."
- "I'm not a manager, but I have such a hard time giving feedback to the colleagues I have to collaborate with. I just don't know how to do it."

Their comments got me thinking. *Why* do so many of the female bosses I've worked with seem to struggle with giving feedback more than their male counterparts? Of course, there is the understandable concern that they'll be perceived as overly harsh or bitchy if they don't sugarcoat the news. But research points to an added factor that lies in how male and female brains function.

There is an emerging field of study looking into the differences between how male and female brains are wired. A 2016 study from the University of Pennsylvania looked at the brain connectivity of two thousand healthy people. They found that female brains typically had far more grey matter in the hippocampus, the part of the brain that plays a role in forming memories, and the left caudate, a part of the brain that controls social cognition. The study concluded that this apportioning of grey matter is why women in general tend to be better at intuiting how others are feeling and knowing how to respond.

This field of research is controversial because of concerns that studies like this can be used to perpetuate stereotypes. It should also be said that not all women have a typical "female brain," and not all men have a typical "male brain." But I do think that this study can help us learn how to make the most of our inherent abilities. When I read about this study, it helped me understand why I had such a hard time confronting Kira. I was intuiting how the negative feedback might make her feel. However, when I changed the way I thought about giving feedback from a critique that would cause her pain to a form of support, my natural empathy actually became an asset because I knew how to respond to ease her pain.

As I learned through my conversation with Kira, when you leverage your kindness to give feedback empathetically, these conversations become more pleasant for everyone involved. In addition, science actually backs up the fact that this approach is more effective. As you'll see in this brief (but interesting!) detour into neurology, this is in part because of the way the human brain works.

Like all animals, humans have a part of the brain called the amygdala. It's like a guard dog sleeping with one eye open, alert for any possible threats. If your amygdala senses a threat, it turns on your body's fight-or-flight response, which sets off a cascade of hormonal reactions that cause you to become angry (fight), want to run away (flight), or shut down, like a deer in a car's headlights (freeze).

The amygdala is meant to protect us when we are confronted by a physical threat, such as the threat of being hit by a car while walking across the street. When you see a car speeding toward you, your amygdala takes over, cutting off access to your more analytic prefrontal cortex. This prompts you to run instinctively and without thinking. That's a good thing. After all, in the face of imminent danger, you don't want to stand there thinking, "Should I run or not? Let me just take a minute to weigh the pros and cons . . ."

Unfortunately, the amygdala isn't very good at distinguishing between real and perceived threats. Our fight-or-flight response can be triggered in all sorts of non-life threatening situations. This is why we often find ourselves in situations where we make comments we regret later (fight), avoid working through a situation (flight), or suddenly disengage mentally, which sometimes means that we will literally not be able to recall what was said (freeze).

According to David Rock, founder of the NeuroLeadership Institute, there are five types of social threats that can trigger this response, all of which you can easily imagine coming up at work:

- Status: a threat to your reputation in the group
- Certainty: a threat to your ability to count on what you thought you could count on
- Autonomy: a threat to your ability to do things your way
- Relatedness: a threat to your sense of yourself as a friend rather than a foe
- Fairness: a threat to your sense of fair play

According to Rock, performance evaluations usually trigger a sense of threat in one or more of these categories, causing someone who receives anything but positive feedback to become angry, feel demotivated, or fail to take in anything you've said to them. But when you tap into your empathy to give constructive feedback, you *avoid* triggering this threat response in the other person. Ultimately, this increases that person's ability to take in what you say, protects your relationship with them, and helps improve an employee's performance without shattering their confidence.

How to Give Empathetic Feedback

In the years since my conversation with Kira, I've given constructive feedback hundreds of times. Along the way, I've learned more and more about how to leverage my empathy and kindness to make these conversations as pleasant and effective as possible.

You can do this by following these steps. And if you're not in a managerial role yet, remember that you can use these same techniques for delivering any type of disappointing or difficult news.

Frame It Positively

Presentation here is everything. Remember, the need to give feedback is not a problem—it's a normal part of the managerial process. So don't frame the conversation in a negative light by saying things like, "Here are some issues I'm seeing in your performance,"

or, "Here are some areas I'm finding that are challenging for you."
Instead, make it clear that you're *not* disappointed in this person.
You're their biggest champion, and you're just trying to help them
succeed even more. You can do this by saying, "I have some advice that might help you," or, "I have some constructive feedback
for you."

To reduce the threat to the other person's status, I always frame
the problem in a positive context by focusing first on what my
team member is doing right. This approach is often referred to as a
"praise sandwich," and it's very effective. Rather than implying, "everything is wrong," I come from the direction of, "a lot is going well,
but there are some things that need improvement." For this reason,
I began my talk with Kira by discussing how great she was at pull-
ing together the financial data. This positive start put her at ease so
that the rest of our conversation could be truly constructive.

I often follow this by allowing the other person to voice the
problem by saying something like, "What are some areas you'd like
to focus on improving?" In many cases, they already know where
they're falling short. When they say it first, it becomes something
we are working on together instead of a criticism that I'm direct-
ing at them.

This practice allows me to shift into my natural state of acting as a mentor and source of support and eliminates any sense of
threat entirely. I tell them straight out, "I want to see you succeed,
and I'm here to support you." This is a strong and motivating position for any authentically kind leader.

Don't Get Personal

I always make sure to separate the person from the situation. In
other words, I can have negative feelings about behavior or performance, but I still need to show empathy and support for the person. This, in turn, causes them to look at the problem from a more
productive and less defensive or guilty perspective.

To get into this objective mindset, I focus on the facts and the behavior I'd like to see in the future instead of making any emotional statements or blaming the other person for what's happened in the past. I also frame my questions carefully. Instead of asking Kira, "What do you think *you* could have done differently?" I asked, "What do you think could have been done differently?"

Jenny Fleiss, the cofounder of Rent the Runway, says, "Starting a critical feedback conversation by asking questions and giving an employee the chance to share thoughts on how he or she feels they have performed upfront has often led to their addressing an issue or topic on their own and ultimately a nicer and more effective outcome." I completely agree, and this subtle change shifts the tone of the conversation from feeling like a personal attack that neither of you wants to be involved in to a more meaningful dialogue.

Provide as Much Context as Possible

Rather than just demanding that an employee redo her work, I always make sure to explain exactly why I'm asking him or her to do something. This is a strategy that I learned from one of my bosses at Time, Inc. who was excellent at giving me the big picture first and then tying in how I could be more effective at supporting that bigger picture. It's so important that an employee understands the "why" behind your feedback, as well as everything you ask him or her to do. This is one way for a boss to keep her team motivated in a kind, yet effective way while striving to meet high standards.

For example, I remember preparing a strategic review with Liz White, who was a crucial member of my team when I was at Time, Inc. When Liz sent me a draft of her presentation, the formatting of the financial section was a bit off. I wanted her to fix it, but I knew this might come across as really nitpicky and annoying.

So instead of giving her a complaint, I gave her the greater context. "If your financials are misaligned or look sloppy, it can give people a lack of confidence in your numbers," I told her. "You don't want to give them any reason to question the numbers." Once she understood exactly *why* this was so important, Liz was happy to fix the formatting issues, and it was something that came more and more naturally to her going forward.

Do It in Person

We're all so busy that it can be extremely tempting to pick up the phone or even just fire off an email to give quick feedback. But I have seen over and over again that it's so important to have these conversations in person. This goes back to the way our brains work. We have specialized brain cells called *mirror neurons* that only fire when we're in the presence of another person. When you are with another person, you observe their behavior and your mirror neurons fire, mirroring that behavior so that you feel as if you have acted in the same way. This process allows us to pick up on the emotional intention of whomever we are speaking to in a way that is simply impossible over the phone or via email.

I've made this mistake myself on more than one occasion. One of my team members named Susan once sent me a press release over email that had a lot of problems. I knew that I should wait and talk to her about it in person, but I was swamped, and I wanted to get it over with, so I just picked up the phone and called her. Even though I followed all of my other advice above, the conversation didn't go well. Susan couldn't sense my empathy or compassion over the phone, and she became upset. But the worst part was that I didn't even notice this at the time because I couldn't read *her* body language, either! It wasn't until I saw Susan's face at a group meeting later that afternoon that I realized how upset she really was.

We're all going a million miles a minute, and it's often so hard to find time to sit down face-to-face, but after what happened with Susan I thought back to the best leaders I'd worked with and found that they all somehow managed to do this. One of my bosses at

Time, Inc. often popped into my office, asked whether I had a spare minute, and dispensed some valuable advice.

My experience with Susan taught me that meeting face-to-face is one of the most important aspects of delivering empathetic feedback and something you can never shortcut. It's the only way to ensure that the other person picks up on your sincerity and kindness. Plus, it leads them to mirror this authenticity. This is where niceness truly feels like a superpower—it causes actual positive changes in other people, just by interacting with them in person. So by being sincere and authentic with people, you are automatically encouraging the same behavior in them, even in the midst of the most challenging conversations. If you work remotely, having these conversations over video conference is better than giving feedback over the phone or, even worse, over email.

Be Specific Without Micromanaging

A huge challenge for some female bosses is to delegate appropriately and give specific feedback without being seen as a micromanager. There is yet another double standard at work here. Author and sociologist BJ Gallagher has observed that the same characteristics that are accepted and even welcomed in male leaders are often resented in female ones. For example, while a male boss is seen as being attentive to details, a female who acts the same way is seen as picky. And as a result, female bosses have an unfair reputation for being micromanagers.

I have seen some female leaders go too far in the other direction to avoid playing into this stereotype. Instead of getting into the nitty-gritty details and risk being accused of micromanaging, they give feedback that's too vague. Over the years, I have learned to strike a balance here by providing specific feedback while focusing on the broad strokes. By that I mean, stating the one or two specific areas where the other person missed the mark without getting too far into the weeds.

Call in the Experts

Sometimes, particular feedback can be so sticky or delicate that it may be better for the other person to hear it from an impartial third party. This is not the same as avoiding the issue. I actually see it as a form of kindness. Some feedback is simply easier to take in when it comes from someone you don't have a relationship with and won't have to face in the office every day.

I had a situation like this with a woman on my team who had been accused of suffering from the dreaded condition we all know as "resting bitch face." Look, this term is sexist in and of itself. I sit in meetings all the time with men who have an angry or dispassion-ate look on their faces, and everyone just assumes they're thinking about something deep and brilliant. But when a woman has a near identical expression, she's viewed as unpleasant and nasty.

Unfortunately, in this case, I had several people from other de-partments coming to me and complaining that this person brought the whole room down with her facial expressions. I was torn. On the one hand, I did not want to force her to change something about herself that a man would never have to worry about. What was I going to do—tell her to smile more? That's so incredibly sex-ist and infuriating. But at the same time, I had to face the fact that this was negatively affecting her performance because people liter-ally did not want her around.

Eventually, I decided to hire a media coach to give my entire team some tips on how to present themselves well in meetings and interviews, and I had a conversation with the coach ahead of time about the feedback I'd received about this particular team member. In this case, I thought it would be too painful (and unfair) for me to deliver this feedback myself, no matter how kind or empathetic I may have been. It would be less insulting coming from a neutral third party who was seen as an expert in this field.

No, I don't believe that women should be sitting in meetings worrying about our facial expressions instead of focusing on being as creative and effective as possible. But in that delicate situation, I had to find the most tactful way possible to let my team member know that she was being judged—however unfairly—by the way she presented herself at work.

Five Nice Ways to Assertively Communicate Bad News

1. Body language matters. Sit up straight and maintain eye contact throughout the conversation, no matter how difficult it may be.
2. Make sure your facial expression matches the content of your conversation. Don't fire someone with a big, fake smile on your face.
3. Begin your sentences with "I."
4. Remember to pause after speaking and to stay silent during those gaps in conversation in order to give the other person time to respond.
5. Be clear on what you want to communicate—and how you'll communicate it—before you go into the conversation. You might even try practicing in front of the mirror or writing out a script.

Balancing Positive to Negative Feedback

Obviously, giving my team positive feedback and praise has always come more naturally to me than sharing constructive feedback. This is where I've been able to really draw on my relational skills to create a bond with my team. But I've had to be careful not to slide toward being a people pleaser by throwing compliments around so much that they become meaningless.

When an authentically nice leader constantly tells her employees how great they are, she may be seen as someone they can walk all over. Throughout my career, I have relied on the following techniques to strike the balance between being positive and supportive yet maintaining high expectations:

- **Take a Ten to One Shot:** My sister Josephine D'Ippolito told me years ago that her boss, the textile designer Carolyn Ray, said that when you're managing people, "You have to give ten 'attaboys' for every one 'aw, shit.'" This doesn't mean that you should literally give ten pieces of praise for every bit of criticism; the idea is that it motivates employees when you make sure the positives outweigh the negatives. I was surprised to find that there is actually research backing this up. A study in the *Harvard Business Review* showed that the highest performing teams received six pieces of praise for every piece of criticism.

- **Be Specific:** Instead of heaping general praise on your team, tell them specifically what you appreciate about their work. For example: "I really like the way you thought that through," or, "I really like that you pressure tested this idea before bringing it to me," or, "I appreciate the fact that you got input from industry thought leaders." Correlate their actions to the results you want. This is not only kind, but also a positive and focused way to motivate your team to do excellent work!

- **Save It:** Be careful not to dilute the impact of your praise by handing it out too much. I try to save my praise for the end of a large project or initiative instead of saying it every day. This is how I balance being nice without being seen as *too* nice or fake. At the end of an initiative, even if the outcome isn't exactly what I wanted, I make sure to praise my team's effort and acknowledge that they did everything they could to get a positive result.

- **Serve It Up Early:** On the other hand, when I have a new person on my team, I like to help them get an early win to boost their confidence. I also encourage my team to do this for each other. This can be something really simple and straightforward. For example, when one of my assistants started at Time, Inc., I realized that we didn't have a team directory. I asked her to put one together with everyone's name, picture, and contact info. It was an easy task, but once it was done, the directory was extremely useful to have. At the next all hands meeting, I shared the directory with the team and said, "Katie put this together; it's going to be really helpful." Everyone clapped, and Katie beamed. I think this moment gave her the confidence to start at her new job with a bang. Moreover, this is the kind of positive action that a boss who undervalues kindness would never think to do. I always think about this when someone tries to tell me that being nice at work is a liability and not an asset!

The Receiving End of Feedback

When I was at Time, Inc., my team wanted to create a new iPhone app for one of our brands, and we needed a financial investment to make it happen. My team put a lot of time and effort into creating a brief presentation that we then took to the CFO and CEO to ask for the money to create the app. The answer was no. I walked out of the room after the pitch meeting with a peer, chatting about what had just happened. I felt defeated and deflated. "We should have presented more comps," I said, but my colleague was undeterred. "I bet we can tweak a few things and go back in and pitch again," he said.

It struck me that I was being too sensitive and too hard on myself. I cared so much about getting it right the first time that I took it badly when things didn't go well. Then I wasted time beating myself up when I could have been moving on to my next win. Sound familiar? This intense emotional investment in our work is a wonderful sentiment, but it can make receiving negative feedback extremely difficult.

I experienced this again in another situation at Time, Inc. when I made the mistake of trying *too* hard to be helpful and low-maintenance. Yes, I admit it—I was being a people pleaser! My boss wanted me to write a strategic plan for one of our brands, and she gave me a couple of months to get it done. I thought I knew what she wanted, and I didn't want to bother her, so I never checked in with her to make sure I was on the right track. Instead, I wrote a forty-page PowerPoint deck all by myself. She looked at it for the first time on the day of the presentation in front of the entire team and said, "This is not what I wanted at all. You totally missed the boat."

I was devastated. I left the room, slammed the door, and went into the bathroom to cry. A friend of mine found me in there and said, "I understand why you're upset, but honestly, you're going to have to develop a thicker skin. It's not personal; it's business."

For me, just hearing those words made all the difference. I was able to learn from this mistake (*of course* I should have checked in with my boss before the day of the presentation!). And just like when I gave feedback to my team, I learned to separate the person from the facts. The fact was that I had screwed up—but that didn't make *me* a screw-up. This was a crucial distinction.

Earlier, I suggested taking the initiative and simplifying spreadsheets and presentations for your boss before showing them to him or her, but this time my mistake was taking *too much* initiative. The difference was, this wasn't just a matter of consolidating information that already existed. I was creating a strategic plan from scratch, which was a huge undertaking. Plus, it was the first time I was doing something like this, so I definitely should have checked in with my boss early on in the process to make sure I was on the right track.

If you're ever in doubt about whether or not to solicit feedback, try asking your boss, "Would you like to see an early version of this before I deliver the final draft?" or, "How often would you like me to check in with you while I'm working on this?"

Over time, this mistake and many others have taught me to develop a growth mindset. Carol Dweck, a professor of psychology at Stanford, differentiates between a growth mindset and a fixed mindset. People who have a growth mindset believe that, through training and hard work, their talents can be developed, while those with a fixed mindset believe that their talents are innate gifts that cannot be changed. Dweck's research shows that people with a growth mindset achieve more because they focus on learning. In many ways, this is a self-fulfilling prophecy. When you believe you *can* get better at something, it's more likely that you will.

When it comes to receiving feedback, then, developing a growth mindset is a huge help. Instead of criticism, it will feel like an opportunity for growth. And whether you're on the giving or receiving end of feedback, it's important to allow your empathy to rise to the surface. When you put yourself in the other person's shoes, you can see that the person critiquing you is merely trying to help.

To Cry . . . Or Not to Cry

A lot has been said and written about women who cry at work—whether or not it's appropriate and if it will be held against you if you do it. I'm not saying it's the best idea, but I'll certainly admit to having cried at work a few times. I've also been the person who other women have cried *to* at work more times than I can count. Afterwards, they often feel guilty, as if they've failed or have shown too much weakness.

I don't think it's a sign of weakness when a woman gets emotional at work. In fact, when my high-performing team members have cried to me, it's shown me how much they really cared about getting it right. That's a good thing. But that doesn't mean that you should cry or vent to your boss over every little mishap.

If you feel yourself getting emotional about feedback you've received or upset about something that happened at work, it's not the end of the world. You can say, "Wow, I really was not expecting that. I need some time to collect myself, but then I would like to talk through this more."

Then, go and call someone you love outside of work and let it out. Don't let your emotions build up inside of you, or they will come out in other ways and hinder your performance. After I've vented to a friend or family member, I feel so much better and can think more clearly about how to continue the conversation in a much more stable and professional way. But I still don't go back right away. Instead, I sleep on it and see how I feel in the morning. Most of the time, I'm already over it by the next day and ready to move on.

If you do this and yet something is still bothering you and it's getting in the way of your contributions, it is important to communicate it. Many of the young women I mentor would never dream of having this type of conversation with their boss, but it's important to stand up for yourself to make sure you can do your best work.

One woman I mentor named Lynne was dealing with a situation just like this. The team she was leading was creating a new program for their online educational software, and they had decided on a feature that was going to be included in the program. But then, without any warning to Lynne, her boss announced to the entire team that they weren't going to include that feature. She felt, and rightly so, that this had undermined her authority with her team, and after taking some distance and venting to her family, she was still very upset about it.

I encouraged Lynne to talk to her boss. She was concerned

about how to do this in a way that would not be perceived as whiny or overly sensitive, so I told her to frame it in the context of why this would prevent her from doing the best job she could for the company and to use all the same techniques I described earlier about how to give feedback empathetically. We sat down and together developed the following script:

"I've been struggling with something that I need to talk to you about. This is not an easy conversation to have with you, but I think it's important for our relationship and for my contributions to the company as a whole. When you told my team that you'd decided not to include the feature in the new program, I felt it undermined my credibility with my team. This makes it difficult for me to be an effective manager if they're going to question my decision-making."

Lynne used this script, and her boss responded positively. In fact, Lynne reported to me later that their relationship was stronger than ever. Her success proved to me that when you allow your empathy to guide you and use the techniques in this chapter to balance it with criticism, you can give kind, yet straightforward feedback to an employee *and* a boss alike. And by adopting a growth mindset, you'll be able to see constructive feedback as a way to develop your own skills even more.

Key Takeaways

- Empathy can be an asset when giving feedback if you balance it with specific comments and context so the other person has a clear understanding of what needs to change and why.
- When giving feedback, remember to let positive reinforcement outweigh negative criticisms. Research shows that the highest-performing teams receive six pieces of praise for every piece of criticism.

- Receiving feedback is an opportunity to grow and develop—
  not a sign of a problem. Instead of beating yourself up for the
  things you haven't done perfectly, focus on how you can truly
  work on improving your performance by using the feedback
  you have received.

5

Make Decisions Firmly *and* Collaboratively

WHEN I THINK ABOUT THE TOUGH DECISIONS I've had to make over my career, one in particular comes to mind. When I was at Time, Inc., we launched a site called StyleFind, a shopping website curated by InStyle editors. It was a big undertaking that required a significant investment of money and resources, but it just didn't work.

For a while, we let it flounder. StyleFind was my baby—I had been the one to ask for all that investment to get it started—and I was worried that if we shut it down I would be seen as a failure, and it would be my scarlet letter. After two years of watching it struggle, I had to decide whether we should invest even more time and resources into StyleFind to try and make it succeed or just cut our losses and let it go.

In addition to worrying about how this decision would affect my own career, I was concerned about how it would affect the company and the rest of my team. I'd always thought that tapping into my natural empathy had given me an edge in business because it helped me build relationships, loyalty, and trust. But now I wondered if, when it came to making tough decisions, empathy was more of a liability.

There is a widely accepted myth that "nice girls" are wishy-washy and have difficulty making decisions because they spend too much time worrying about what other people think. It's true that because we have empathy for others, we are keenly aware of how our actions impact them and their lives. But that's not necessarily a bad thing. In fact, it can be an enormous strength as a leader if wielded strategically

The trick here, of course, is to strike a balance between being empathetic and being a worrier, unable to call the shots because you're so worried about how your decisions will affect others. Yes, it's essential to think everything through from multiple perspectives and collect buy-in and advice from colleagues. But at the end of the day, a leader has to be able to stand in his or her own shoes, make a clear decision, and then own the results of that decision. As I mentioned earlier, empathy turning into worry is definitely my Achilles' heel, and so throughout my career it has been especially important for me to develop concrete and well-planned strategies to help me act more decisively.

This is not easy, and I know plenty of others who have struggled with this, as well. Take a look at what some of the women I surveyed had to say:

- "I think that women who are decisive get unfairly labeled as bossy, so I tend to shy away from making big decisions at work."
- "I like to ask a lot of people for their opinions before making a decision, but then I worry that people will hold it against me if I don't take their advice."
- "Sometimes I think that if I ask for advice, I'll be seen as weak or ineffective, so I try to make most of my decisions without seeking any input from others. But I wonder if I could be making more informed decisions if I did it another way."

Develop Evidence-Based Confidence

To make tough decisions, you need to have the confidence that you are capable of making a smart, informed, and effective choice. A lot has been written about women and confidence, but I've noticed that there are two key components lacking from that discussion: a clear idea of where confidence comes from and what distinguishes confidence from ego.

True confidence is not something that you are simply born with. It's a skill you can develop by paying close attention to your successes in life and how you accomplished them. This purposeful self-reflection will result in the type of evidence-based confidence that does not come across as arrogant or pushy. On the other hand, when someone is full of self-importance and walks around believing that they are just generally wonderful without seeming to need real evidence to back it up, well, that's not confidence— that's just ego.

Several years ago, I was interviewing with an influential woman who commented that I had a "quiet self-confidence." At first, I wasn't sure what she meant or whether it was even a compliment! Was she saying that I was demure and passive? That wasn't what I wanted to project. But she explained that she wanted people on her team who would contribute significantly without letting their egos get in the way. As I listened, I realized that she was describing the type of confidence that's grounded in experience.

To this day, when I'm struggling with a decision or feeling insecure, I go back to the evidence. Not long ago, I was giving a big speech to three hundred managers, and I was quite nervous. A close friend told me, "Think back and remember a time when you gave a good speech." It was simple but solid advice. Before delivering that big presentation, I thought back to a speech I'd given a few years before that my team said had really resonated with them. I visualized that speech in as much detail as I could possibly remember—what I'd said, how I said it, and what it had felt like to succeed. This made me feel far more confident.

When I was facing the decision of whether or not to shut down StyleFind, I remembered this mental approach. I thought back to tough decisions I'd made in the past that ended up having great outcomes, and I examined the process I'd used to make those decisions. I realized that in every case, I'd taken in all of the necessary data and then ended up going with my gut. Not my brain, not my heart, but my gut. That was the process that worked for me, and knowing that allowed me to move forward using that technique to make a decision with confidence.

Many other leaders also tap into evidence-based confidence to make tough decisions. My friend Mindy Grossman, currently the CEO of Weight Watchers, took a very public risk when she took HSNI (the parent company of HSN and Cornerstone Brands) public back when she was their CEO in 2008, just as the economic meltdown was unfolding. Mindy had to convince consumers, employees, and the board to take a chance with her. She told me that she never could have done that if she hadn't already built a solid network of people who believed in her. This is where being authentically kind and transparent paid off in a big way for Mindy. These people trusted her and were willing to take a major risk with her.

Still, when the time came closer, Mindy admitted that she had some fears. She told me that she remembers standing out on the terrace thinking, "Can I do this? Six thousand employees are counting on me." In that moment, Mindy went back to her evidence-based confidence. She reminded herself of all the detailed due diligence she had done before making the decision to move ahead. Reflecting on all of that hard work gave her the inner confidence to believe in herself and what she was doing.

To develop your own evidence-based confidence, ask yourself the following questions:

- "When have I done something difficult . . . and survived?"
- "When have I made wise choices?"
- "What process have I used when making successful decisions?"

Then move forward making your decision with confidence by using the following techniques:

Fill In the Gaps

It's obviously important to seek advice from others when making a decision, but how many people and specifically which ones?

It turns out that there are physiological differences in the ways women and men respond to stressful situations. (And yes, having to make a tough decision at work can certainly trigger a stress response.) While men typically go into fight-or-flight mode when faced with a stressor, women tend to seek out social groups during times of stress. Psychologists refer to this as the "tend and befriend" stress response. Studies show that women's brains release more of a hormone called oxytocin in response to stress than men's. Oxytocin makes us feel good about social interaction, causing women to seek out friends during times of stress.

In part because of this response to stress, many of us go to our closest friends and family members when facing a tough decision. But are they really best equipped to give you an informed opinion? Not always. Instead of going to those closest to me, the first thing I do when making a decision is to try and figure out what kind of expertise I'm currently missing. Then I put together a team I can call on for advice that fills the gaps in my experience and knowledge. This allows me to hear multiple perspectives, but in a focused and purposeful way that doesn't delay or derail my decision-making.

I've often shared this strategy to help other women avoid the pitfall of seeking input from too many people. When one of the female startup founders I was working with recently as an advisor had a big decision to make, she went to dozens of investors (mostly male) for advice. Not only was this extremely time-consuming, but it was also off-target. The product she was developing was an app geared toward young girls. And the men she'd gone to for advice didn't really get what she was doing and gave her conflicting and often overly critical advice. This left her doubting her decisions and completely stuck.

I told her, "This is where you have to be the boss. You started this company, so you get to decide whom you are going to listen to. Does it make sense for you to listen to advice from people who are not your target demographic or experts in what you're trying to do?" I explained that when it comes to seeking advice, more is not necessarily better. Instead, it's important to be strategic about who you seek advice from.

Together, we devised a list of three types of expertise she needed: someone who knew the existing market for her target age group, someone with a background in building new technologies, and someone who really knew how to market to young girls. The advice she received from these three experts was much more in line with her plans and allowed her to make an informed decision that she felt confident about. Ultimately, feeling confident in your decisions should be the goal of every woman who wants to be inclusive and decisive.

In contrast to this founder, I've observed some women fight their instincts to "tend and befriend" and try to make decisions without seeking any outside opinions. They want to appear strong and confident, and of course they don't want to bother anyone by taking up his or her time, so as a result, they act unilaterally. But in reality, acting alone is simply impractical. No one expects you to already know everything. Even the most experienced world leaders still have gaps in their knowledge, and they call in the experts when making tough decisions. That's what we should be doing, too.

Don't ever feel like you're putting yourself in a weak position by asking for help. As a boss, whenever junior members of my team came to me with an idea or opinion and backed it up by saying that they had spoken to an expert beforehand, it struck me as being resourceful and smart. If anything, seeking outside expertise adds strength to your argument, not weakness.

Have a Go-To Team

The people you pull in to round out your knowledge may vary from decision to decision. But it's just as important to have two or three people whom you know you can turn to for advice about anything. These people aren't necessarily experts in this particular area. Instead, they are individuals who know your values intimately and can help keep you grounded. They'll ask the tough questions that will really force you to think. The important thing here is to keep this team small (three to four people, maximum) and make sure they'll give you honest feedback, help you stand strong in your own opinions, and encourage you to stand up and do the right thing.

My go-to team consists of my husband, my dear friend and former colleague Patricia Karpas, and my business coach MJ Ryan, whom I've been working with for seven years. For me, this is a good balance because it consists of someone who knows me personally (my husband), someone who has worked with me (Patricia), and someone who is deeply invested in my business goals and priorities (MJ). Earlier in my career, when I did not have a business coach, I relied on a mentor to fill this role. I never know which member of my go-to team will end up asking the questions that will spark my ultimate decision.

When I was at Time, Inc., I had to let several employees go on the same day as part of a restructuring. This was one of the hardest things I've ever had to do. That morning, I reached out to each of the employees who were being let go and set up a time to meet with them that same day so they weren't left waiting for too long, wondering if it was bad news. Then I had each conversation in that person's own office so they had the comfort of being on their own turf, and I could leave them in peace to collect their thoughts after the conversation was over. At the start of each meeting, I said, "I have some bad news," to let them know right away what was happening, and then I simply shared the news and listened to their reaction.

These conversations were difficult, and I was also worried about how the rest of the team would react. Yes, they still had their jobs, but restructuring is stressful for everyone. I wasn't sure how to communicate with the rest of the team that was left behind after the layoffs were done. The way I saw it, I had three options: I could let each individual manager handle it with their team; I could say and do nothing and simply wait for the CEO to send out a company-wide email; or I could gather everyone in the room at the end of the day and talk with them about what had happened.

That third option would definitely be the most difficult after a draining day, but when I spoke to MJ, she said, "Fran, think about what kind of leader you are and what's most important to you." I immediately knew that, since building solid relationships was one of my core values, the most authentic thing for me would be to pull everyone together and talk directly with them.

Make no mistake: it was still difficult to face the room. But making this decision ahead of time made it easier for me because I had my talking points planned and practiced before I went into the room. And having the emotional support and validation that came from talking it over with someone I trusted helped me feel confident about what I was doing. This ended up being the right decision because it allowed me to protect my relationships with my remaining team, help them feel secure in their jobs, and make sure they remained emotionally invested in the company.

Pull In the Stakeholders

As a leader, I've found it effective to get input from the people who will be directly affected by my decisions, even if they are more junior than me. There have been times in my career when people have accused me of being "too nice" for doing this. They said I would appear weak if I gave the individuals who reported to me too much input, but I saw it differently. To me, my team consisted of stakeholders who were totally invested in my decisions. I was liable to them. So I always got their input while still making it clear that, in the end, the ultimate decision would rest with me.

A woman I advised named Vanessa was recently setting up the office space for the company she'd founded, and she'd hired a consultant to design an open floor plan for her forty-person staff. Vanessa asked my opinion on the floor plan, and my first question to her was, "Have you asked your staff what they think? They're the ones who will be working in this environment every day."

Vanessa resisted this idea at first. She thought she would be seen as a pushover if she asked for their input. I told her instead to think of her staff as a focus group and to ask one person from each department. She followed my advice and ended up gaining some significant suggestions. In particular, the representative from the sales department noted that they'd need private space in order to feel comfortable making sales calls. So Vanessa added several private offices to the open floor plan for the sales team to duck into to make calls. Her team ended up being far more productive because they had what they needed to succeed and felt that they'd been heard. Far from being seen as a pushover, Vanessa was able to be inclusive *and* decisive and actually gain respect from her team.

Once you make the decision, thank everyone you've consulted for his or her input. Acknowledge that your decision is not going to make everyone happy, but express that you feel strongly that it's the right direction. And at the end of the day, it's better to make a decision so you can all move on.

Own It—For Now

One thing that has made it hard at times for me to make decisions is my concern that I'd have to stick by my decision forever or else I'd be perceived as wishy-washy.

This happened frequently when I first started working with my team at Time, Inc. on developing new apps. The technology was changing so quickly that we often had to go back on decisions that had already been made, such as which features to include in the final product. Working with new technologies forced me to become more comfortable with things changing quickly. This experience helped me make quick decisions and own them while remaining aware that these calls didn't have to be forever. In short, I learned to embrace change.

Things in life are constantly changing—not just technology, but also internal dynamics and politics—and sometimes it makes sense to revisit previous decisions down the road. Contrary to unhelpful myths, doing so does not make you weak or wishy-washy; rather, it makes you decisive *and* flexible, which is an important balance for a leader to strike.

When you make a decision, own it. Never apologize for your decision—even if you have to revisit it later or the results are not what you wanted. When I've made a decision that didn't garner positive results, I've said, "We made the best decision we could based on the facts at the time, but given where we are now as a company and what our goals are, we now need to revisit this decision."

How to Cut Your Losses

After agonizing over what to do about StyleFind, I used the decision-making technique that I knew worked best for me. I looked at the numbers (which proved once and for all that it was failing) and listened to my gut, which told me to let it go. I finally ended up suggesting that we shut down StyleFind. It was a failure, but instead of dwelling on that, I looked back to see what we could have done differently.

I realized that when we were launching StyleFind, we were never able to incorporate the consumer value proposition (a statement that describes why a customer should buy a product or use a service) into its marketing and tagline, and that was one of the main reasons it failed. The fact that it wasn't easy for one consumer to concisely communicate the product's benefits to another was something that had bothered me about StyleFind from the very beginning.

Later, I was able to bring what I'd learned from StyleFind to my work as an investor. I became very sensitive to how easy or difficult it is for a founder to communicate the consumer value proposition. When I sense that clearly marketing a product's benefits will be a problem, I see it as a red flag, and I usually don't invest. This strategy has helped me identify the most promising companies to invest in, and I never would have known it if not for the hard lessons I learned from my experience with StyleFind.

As an investor and advisor, I have seen many women struggle with this inability to cut their losses because they fear being seen as a failure. It takes guts and confidence to cut your losses, but this is often the best way of staying afloat instead of going down with the ship.

I was so impressed when Blake Lively, whose company, Preserve, I had invested in, decided to shutter the company. Blake told *Vogue*, "I never thought I would have the bravery to actually do that, to take the site dark and to say, 'You know what? I haven't created something that is as true and impactful as I know it can and will be. And I'm not going to continue to chase my tail and continue to put a product out there that we, as a team, are not proud of.'"

Reading that, do you see Blake as a failure who should never be given another chance . . . or as a strong leader who is going to bounce back bigger and better than ever? She knows that I will want to hear her next business idea, and my bet is that she will be an even stronger founder the second time around.

So how do you know when is the best time to cut your losses? Of course, you don't want to go to the other extreme and give up on something too soon, either. When you're unsure about which way to go, think about what would need to happen to turn things around and make this venture a success. You can usually boil it down to three to four variables. Then ask yourself what the probability of success is on each of those variables. If that probability is low, it's time to cut your losses, but if not, you still have a good chance of success.

For example, I boiled StyleFind's likelihood of success down to these three variables:

1. We would have to make it a bigger part of InStyle.com, which was unlikely since there were other features of the site that were performing better.
2. Google would have to change its algorithm. One key factor that was hurting us was that Google had changed its algorithm, and we were getting less traffic than we'd expected. This was an external influence that was completely out of our control.
3. We would need a big marketing budget from the company. I knew that it wasn't the right time to make this ask because the company was looking to cut costs, not do more investing.

Looking at these three variables and how low the probability of success was for all three, it was clear that it was time to let StyleFind go.

How to Get Unstuck When You Are Making a Decision

Even if you follow all of the preceding advice, chances are at some point you'll face a decision that, for one reason or another, is really difficult for you to make. When this happens, these are my go-to techniques:

1. Take a step back and think about the bigger picture. It's really easy to get too deep into the weeds, especially when you are stuck. If it's a choice between two options, ask yourself which option is more closely aligned with your overall vision and values (or those of the company).

2. Find someone who has dealt with a similar issue in the past and talk to them about how they made the decision. It may be someone in your company or at a different company. Don't reinvent the wheel — most likely, someone else has already put a lot of thought into this. Tap into that knowledge to inform your own decision.

3. Visualize what your world would look like if you said yes. I recently was offered a CEO role, which my ego was obviously very attracted to. But then I started visualizing what my day-to-day would look like . . . a two hour commute each day to a high-pressure job, which would mean less time with my kids and on other projects that are meaningful to me. (More on this in Chapter 8.)

4. Give yourself a break and stop thinking about it for a while. Often the best solution comes when you create headspace for yourself, like when you are taking a walk or in the shower!

Take the Emotions Out of Your Decisions

My friend Chrissy Carter, who left a career on Wall Street to become a yoga teacher, has taught me so much about balancing empathy and other emotions with the need to make tough decisions. On Wall Street, Chrissy found that she had to react quickly and be very precise, while her natural inclination was to take a lot of time to contemplate and consider things from all sides before making a final decision. It was a challenge for her to quickly sift through her emotions in order to arrive at a clear decision, but she became more proficient at it the more she practiced.

Chrissy learned to identify the signs that she was having an emotional reaction to an email or a piece of news and would strategically wait before responding. Then, after a day or two, she'd play "Monday morning quarterback" by going back to the conversation or message that upset her to figure out what triggered her. The more she did this, the quicker she caught herself when she was being triggered in real time. Then, she could take that emotional reaction off the table and have a professional conversation or make a quick decision.

Here are the steps she uses to take her emotions out of workplace decision-making:

- Identify your visceral reactions to a trigger, which could include a knot in your stomach, tension in your throat, or a tightening of your jaw. Be aware of these sensations.
- When you feel those physical sensations, consciously choose *not* to take any action at that moment.
- Later, go back and write out what happened like it was a scene in a play. What was said right before you felt that visceral reaction? Why do you think you reacted this way?
- As you become more aware of what triggers you, you'll be able to recognize when you need to take a step back and try to approach the situation with some objective clarity.

Failure, Confidence, and Risk

Obviously, making the decision to shut down StyleFind did not end up destroying my career, as I'd feared. In fact, I recall one senior executive saying to me, "No one bats a thousand. Failure comes with the territory." But when it happens, it can really shake your confidence. Understandably, we often interpret a serious setback as evidence of our inability to lead, and that makes us feel insecure.

It's interesting to note how women in particular react to failure. The *Harvard Business Review* found that women were far less likely to apply for a leadership role if they had been turned down for a similar role in the past. Over time, this is undoubtedly one of the factors keeping women out of senior management roles. How can we become more comfortable risking failure and rejection?

In their book *Art & Fear*, David Bayles and Ted Orland tell a story about a ceramics teacher who conducted an experiment. He divided a beginner's pottery class in half and told the people on one side that they'd be graded on *quantity*. The more pots they produced, the better their grade would be. Then he told the other half that they'd be graded on *quality*. The more perfect their pot, the better their grade would be.

Guess which group made better pots? The one that was focused on quantity. Why? Because they practiced. *Because they failed.* And they ultimately improved their technique through trial and error. The group that was hung up on perfection never took risks, so they never failed, and, as a result, they never learned or improved.

I recently heard that 80% of women CEOs played team sports in high school and college. This data made perfect sense to me. In playing a team sport, women learn how not to take the team's success or failure personally. You win some, you lose some, and then you get back out there on the field the next day. Doing this over and over clearly gave those women CEOs the resilience they needed to catapult themselves to the top.

Even if you think it's too late for you to join a varsity soccer team, it's never too late to learn how to cultivate the confidence to take risks. I recently helped a woman I mentor named Kathryn make a big decision about whether or not to take a risk in her career. Kathryn worked as a pharmaceutical sales representative and was offered a job as a sales manager. It was a promotion with a significant salary increase, but it meant moving from Chicago, where she lived with her husband and son, to North Carolina.

Kathryn and I walked through the potential risks. Her son had special needs, so it was important to find the right school for him. She felt that disrupting him when he was doing well in school was a big risk. Kathryn's husband worked for the same company she did, and they had offered him a position in North Carolina, too, so his job wasn't at stake. But Kathryn was still worried about how the move would affect him. In addition, her family and her husband's family lived in the Midwest. Their entire support system was there.

On the positive side, Kathryn had been bored with her job for the past year or so and was really excited about advancing her career. This promotion was a great opportunity for her to move up and take on more responsibilities. She knew that these opportunities didn't come along often. Once we had a clear sense of the potential risks and rewards, I walked her through the following questions:

- *What would I do if my husband and son weren't a factor?* Of course Kathryn did need to consider how the move might affect her family, but it was also important for her to know what her decision would be otherwise. For Kathryn, it was clear that she would take the new job if she weren't worried about how it would affect her family.
- *What would I do if they were excited for me?* Kathryn was lucky to have a supportive partner who was truly excited for her, but this is not always the case. Imagining what the decision would be like without the pressure of pleasing others can be really helpful for someone (like me) who overdoes it on empathy.
- *Is this decision aligned with my values?* It may sound silly,

but many of us walk through life unsure of what is most important to us. Is it money, fulfillment, love, or something else? Those of us who tend to be people pleasers often forget our own values on our quest to make everyone else happy. But when you have a deep understanding of your core values, it's much easier to make a decision that is aligned with what you cherish most. Kathryn realized that she valued her career and believed that she would be a better mom if she were happier at work.

- *What is the worst-case scenario?* Identifying the worst thing that could happen helps eliminate the fear of the unknown. In the absolute worst-case scenario, Kathryn would hate her new job, her son would be miserable in his new school and stop progressing, and her husband would resent her for making them move. Not a pretty picture, but it was helpful to Kathryn to face it head-on.

- *How can I mitigate the risk?* There is often a way to lessen the impact of your personal risk. Sometimes when "nice girls" are given an opportunity, they hesitate to ask for more because they're afraid of being seen as greedy. But it's smart, not greedy, to seek out what you need in order to mitigate your risk. Kathryn was able to negotiate with her company to get an equivalent job in Chicago if the new position didn't work out within a year. She also was able to rent out her home in Chicago instead of selling it and rent an apartment in North Carolina.

Get Rejected on Purpose

I once heard Sara Blakely, the founder of Spanx, talk about how her father encouraged her to fail as a young child. At the dinner table, he would ask Sara and her brother, "How did you fail today?" Sara credited this freedom to fail with giving her the confidence to take risks that have really paid off for her career. This story really stuck with me, and I can see doing this with my own sons when they're a little bit older.

I also saw a TED talk by Jia Jiang, who went out and intentionally got rejected every day for one hundred days in an effort to overcome his fear of rejection. He literally walked up to strangers and asked them if he could borrow $100 and requested a "burger refill" after finishing his lunch. This may sound silly, but he grew more and more comfortable with being rejected. As a happy side benefit, he also found that many people were kinder than he'd ever imagined.

So if you're scared of taking risks because you might fail or get rejected, why not try it? Ask yourself, *"How am I going to fail today?"* You never know how it will end up helping you succeed.

The Downside of Risk — Dealing with Failure

The truth is that no matter how confident you are or how much you prepare, not every risk you take is going to turn out exactly how you'd like. Take it from me. The biggest career risk I've ever taken didn't work out at all the way I expected it to.

I was still at Time, Inc. when I realized that my side hustle — startup investing and advising — was something I really enjoyed. My two boys were really little at the time, so I was looking for more flexibility at work. I had been in corporate media for fifteen years at that point and felt like it was time to mix it up and do something a little different.

Before making any moves, I spent a lot of time thinking about what I most enjoyed about what I was currently doing. The answer was that I loved meeting startup founders and working closely with them as an advisor and mentor. It was my favorite part of the job, and yet, it was something I was mostly doing for free.

I was still mulling whether I should make the move to becoming a full-time investor when I met Mike Rothenberg. Mike was running a venture capital (VC) fund that I ended up investing in. We got along really well, and he asked me to work for him. This would mean taking a huge risk, and naturally I worried about everything —from how the decision would affect other people in my life to what would happen if I failed.

To make this crucial decision, I asked myself the same questions I had walked through with Kathryn:

- *What would I do if other people weren't a factor?* In my case, my husband was very supportive of the potential move, and I already knew it would be a good choice for my boys because I'd get to spend more time with them if I left my job at Time. I was concerned, though, that my loyal team at Time might feel that I was abandoning them if I moved on. But when I asked myself what I would do if they weren't a factor, the honest answer was that I would take the risk and leave.
- *What if they were excited for me?* Imagining my team at Time being excited for me to embark on this new journey gave me a shot of real confidence to make that decision. It also helped me to see this decision in a new light—as me walking toward a new opportunity *instead* of walking away from something.
- *Is this decision aligned with my values?* At that stage of my career, my boys were my top priority. I also cared about staying relevant in my career. Working in VC would give me more time with my kids, and I knew it would be good for my relevancy because I'd be learning about emerging technologies and expanding my network.
- *What is the worst-case scenario?* The worst-case scenario was that the position wouldn't work out and I would be on my own without a platform. I also knew that my move from Time, Inc.

into the VC world would probably be covered in the media, so it would be embarrassing if it didn't work out.

- *How can I mitigate the risk?* For me, this was perhaps the most important question because it made me see that I could continue doing my own personal startup investing even while working for Mike. That way, if the move didn't go well, I'd still have my own portfolio.

After answering all of these questions and doing my due diligence about Mike and his firm, I found it was much easier to make the decision. I went to work for Mike, and at first, I loved it. I was getting plugged into an incredible network in Silicon Valley, and I really enjoyed being around the enthusiasm of a youthful, energetic team.

I imagined that I would work at Rothenberg Ventures, Mike's VC fund, for a few years and then move onto a larger VC firm. But that's not the way it happened. After two years, I was left feeling disillusioned with VC. I found that my values were increasingly at odds with my day-to-day duties, and I realized that I would be happier investing my own money in startups instead of investing other people's money. This was when I was so glad I had thought about how to mitigate risk and had continued investing on my own. By then, I had built up a personal portfolio of seventeen companies, and I was able to leave Rothenberg without having to worry about what was next.

In the end, the experience didn't go exactly how I'd planned or how I would've hoped, but if I could go back and make a different decision, I wouldn't choose to. It was still the right decision at the time, and I gained so many positives from the experience. I have relationships with people I never would have met otherwise; I have opportunities to speak to large groups of key people that I didn't have before; and it allowed me to develop my own personal brand. It also gave me the time and flexibility to write this book and to work on personal passion projects, like *Girl Starter*, a new reality show about female entrepreneurs.

Just because I wouldn't change my decision doesn't mean that I didn't make mistakes along the way. For one, I should really have taken my own advice and cut my losses even sooner once I realized the position was not a good fit. But I didn't want to feel like I'd failed at this big new venture. It wasn't until after I summoned my confidence, cut my losses, and left that I was able to see that it wasn't a failure because I had gained so much from the experience.

Bottom line? If you take a risk and it doesn't go as planned, welcome to the club. Here's how you can best get up, dust yourself off, and move forward:

Ask yourself:

- "What did I gain from this experience?"
- "If I could go back in time, what would I do differently?"
- "What will I do differently next time?"

Key Takeaways

- True confidence comes from solid evidence of your previous successes, not ego. To develop evidence-based confidence, ask yourself what process you've used in the past to make wise choices.
- Women have a unique stress response to "tend and befriend." To make the most of this instinct, form a go-to team to run tough decisions by. These should only be people you trust, who always encourage you to be your best and to stand up for yourself. It's also helpful to discuss decisions with people who have specific expertise and who've had experiences that you're lacking.
- Women are more likely to become strong leaders if they learn how to take risks and fail on the playing field. To get comfortable with risk, try taking a small risk every day or make a re-

quest that you know is likely to be met with a "no." The more you do this, the more comfortable with and less intimidated by failure you'll become.

- When you find yourself becoming emotional at work, take a step back and think about what preceded this feeling that might have triggered you. When you become aware of those triggers, you can learn when you need to take a moment before being able to make clear decisions that are free of emotion.
- To avoid over-empathizing to the detriment of your own success, when making a decision, ask yourself what you would do if all the people in your life supported your decision.

6

Negotiate with Strategy *and* Empathy

Bridging the Wage Gap

As WE ALL KNOW, THE GENDER WAGE GAP IS real, and it's probably not going away any time soon. In 2015 (the latest year we have data for), there was an overall 20% gap between men's and women's salaries. In other words, on average, women earned eighty cents for every man's dollar. While women have definitely made some progress over the past few decades, the rate of change has now stalled. At the rate of change between 1960 and 2001, women would reach pay equity in 2059, but at the stalled rate since 2001, we won't reach equity until 2152.

The gap is even wider for women of color. In 2015, African American women earned sixty-three cents for every man's dollar while Hispanic or Latina women earned only fifty-four. If you don't think this is affecting you yet, unfortunately all you have to do is wait. On average, women earn 90% of men's salaries until the age of thirty-five, and then the wage gap begins to widen as we get older regardless of race or education levels.

Pretty alarming, isn't it? But what's causing this? A study from 2012 proved that stereotypes and biases are one major cause of the wage gap. In that experiment, science professors who were hiring a lab manager were presented with two resumes that were identical except for one key difference—one had the name John while the other had the name Jennifer. "John" was judged to be more competent and hirable than "Jennifer." And here's the kicker: the professors ultimately offered him a starting salary that was about 12% higher than Jennifer's.

If that's not infuriating enough, think about this—you don't even have to be human to be financially penalized for being female. In a 2014 study, participants were asked to estimate how much they would pay for two identically performing robots—one named Julie and one named James. The robot named James was deemed to be worth a whopping 25% more than Julie. Crazy, right?

I've seen in my own career how stereotypes can cause men to be valued more than women. Earlier on in my career, I was working on the board of a nonprofit doing a compensation review. Every year, the board went through each member of the management team and decided what his or her compensation would be for the following year. We were talking about potential salary increases for a man and a woman who were peers, and an older woman on the board recommended a higher salary increase for the man, explaining that he was the primary breadwinner in his family, while the woman was single and didn't have the same financial stress.

Thankfully, a man on the board spoke up and said, "That's not something we should assume or factor into our decision-making. It looks to me like they're pretty equal in terms of performance and the value they bring to the organization." The rest of the board agreed and decided to give them the same salary increase.

This was the first time I had actually heard someone so explicitly use traditional gender roles as a reason a man should receive a higher salary than a woman who was his equal, and I was shocked. It was particularly disheartening to hear a woman perpetuating this stereotype and actually advocating for the man to receive a higher salary purely because of his gender. I knew that these biases existed, of course, but this experience proved to me how deeply ingrained they were and that they were actively holding women back. At the same time, the outcome gave me hope. I was impressed that the man on the board had stepped up to do the right thing. This showed me that there are men out there who are committed to fighting for equality, and the importance of speaking up when facing these types of situations.

The Negotiating Gap

Besides speaking up for other women when we're at the table and have an opportunity to do so, what can we do to keep shrinking the wage gap? Some of the world's most successful and inspiring women argue that we must do a better job of negotiating our salaries in order to close this gap.

To some extent, I agree with this stance. There are proven differences in the way men and women negotiate or, rather, in whether we do it at all. A recent study of MBA graduates found that half of the male graduates negotiated their first job offers, while only an eighth of the women chose to negotiate. This means that almost 90% of the women very likely left money on the table. As a result, according to this study, the men had starting salaries that were an average of 7.6% higher than the women's.

I have been just as guilty of this as those female MBA graduates. Over the first nine years of my career, I either received a promotion or changed jobs five separate times, and every time, I took the first salary that was offered to me. I was always so grateful to have the job that it never even occurred to me to negotiate.

Now I know that the first offer a company makes is often not their best possible offer. There are normally salary ranges that employers are willing to give for each position. Their first offer may be at the bottom of that range, leaving room to negotiate higher. So if you take the initial offer, there's a good chance that you're missing out.

Speaking to recruiters is one good way to stay on top of the market—to see where there is "heat," which areas are expanding, and which are contracting. This, by the way, is also a way to add value to your company in your current role. Understanding market forces leads to better decisions at all levels of an organization. (I offer more tips on connecting to recruiters in Chapter 7.)

The first time I negotiated my salary was eight years into my career when I left Coke for Moviefone, and even then it was by accident! When I told Coke that I was leaving, they countered in an effort to get me to stay. The counteroffer from Coke was so tempting that I went back to Moviefone and told them that I was now considering staying. To my surprise, Moviefone stepped up and offered more than Coke's counteroffer. Realizing that I had successfully, if unintentionally, negotiated a better deal in terms of salary, bonuses, and stock options, I ended up making the move.

After this enlightening experience, it struck me that I hadn't actually needed Coke to counter in the first place. I could have negotiated with Moviefone right from the beginning based on my own merits—and I realized that I could have been doing that all along in my previous jobs. This was a pivotal moment for me. I had finally learned my value. Going forward, I always made sure to review my compensation package thoroughly instead of accepting it by default and negotiated with confidence when I felt it was appropriate.

As I moved forward in my career, I saw that many of the young women who worked for me were making the same mistakes I had —they didn't negotiate as a matter of course. This became so predictable that I began to expect and even plan for it when I prepared my annual performance reviews with my team. When preparing salary increases ahead of these reviews, I was careful to focus on performance, but even then, I was aware that the men on my team were more likely to negotiate, and sometimes they did end up getting more than their female counterparts who usually did not negotiate.

So *why* are women so much less likely to negotiate? In my experience, it goes back to the people-pleasing mentality that is so easy for women to feel pressured into. Many women worry that they'll come across as aggressive, pushy, or even greedy if they negotiate for themselves. This concern is certainly something I can relate to personally. And I hate to say it, but it turns out there is research to prove that this worry is valid!

In a 2011 study at Emory University, managers were told they would have to discuss raises with their employees. In this case, they offered the men on their teams raises that were two and a half times higher than those they offered to women with equal skills and experience. This was before any negotiations had even begun. But when the same managers were told they would *not* have to justify or discuss the amount of the raise, they offered male and female employees equal raises across the board.

In other words, these managers didn't feel comfortable low-balling male employees when they would be forced to talk about it. They assumed that in their discussions the men would fight harder for higher salaries than the women. So they gave them more from the get-go—*two and a half times more*. And this was despite the fact that they knew the men were not truly worth more—as proved by the equal increases they gave when there was no discussion required.

Once negotiations start, things often get even worse for women. In a series of studies out of Harvard and Carnegie Mellon, evaluators were asked to rank potential employees based on whom they would most like to work with. Both male and female evaluators consistently ranked a woman lower if she had previously initiated negotiations for a higher salary. The same judgment was not inflicted on the men who had negotiated.

In a follow-up, the evaluators themselves were asked if they would have negotiated if they had been the employees in the same scenario, and most of the women said no. But they weren't just being meek or people pleasers; they knew full well that they'd be penalized for negotiating. I believe this is why so many women fail to negotiate for themselves—we're aware of the unfair judgment we face and decide it's ultimately not worth it.

How to negotiate successfully without being penalized for being "pushy" is one of the questions I'm asked the most by women I mentor, and this topic clearly resonated with the women I surveyed. Here's what they had to say:

- "I am a freelancer, so I constantly have to negotiate, and I hate it. It doesn't come naturally to me, and I always feel like I'm being unfairly judged just for asking for what I'm worth."

- "When I took my new job, I didn't negotiate, and I found out later that a male peer negotiated for a similar position and is making over 20% more than me! It makes me feel resentful every day, but I'm not sure what I can do about it now."

- "Although I was uncomfortable doing it, I forced myself to negotiate hard for my current job, and I got the salary and package I wanted, but my male boss still makes cutting remarks three years later about how I'm 'draining his pockets.'"

Nice *and* Strategic Job Negotiation Tactics

So what should we do about all of this? Most of the advice offered to women on this topic is to try to be tough and negotiate "like a man." But my advice is a little different. I think it's important for us to be aware of the biases we are facing, and instead of plowing ahead and negotiating aggressively or failing to negotiate altogether, it's essential to use our relational skills to negotiate strategically in a way that is good for the people on both sides of the table. Here's how:

Focus on Communal Benefits

Studies have shown that women who negotiate communally, meaning with an eye toward what is best for the organization instead of just what is best for themselves, have a better chance of success. This means that in addition to discussing why you deserve the promotion and salary increase, you should talk about how your talents and experiences will add value to the company. For example, "The talents and network that I bring to the table are critical for the company to meet its biggest goals."

Is this a way of playing to a stereotype because women are typically expected to think of others instead of themselves? I don't think so. You're still speaking up for your achievements and asking for what you're worth, but just doing it in a way that gives you the best chance of success. There's nothing submissive about that.

Know Your Value

If you feel uncomfortable negotiating on your own behalf, knowing exactly what you're worth according to the market can help you feel more confident. This can be difficult in companies that are not transparent about salaries and other benefits, but there are other ways to find out what you're worth. From early on in my career, it's been my impression that men talk to each other about money much more than women. But the more we're willing to have open conversations about our worth, the more we can work to close the wage gap.

It took me a long time to get to know my own value as an advisor. For a while, I asked for nothing in return for my time and advice. I'd go to meeting after meeting, sharing my advice for free. Finally, a good friend who also does some advising said to me, "Fran, why are you doing all this work for free? I usually do one introductory meeting at no charge. After that, if people want my advice, they have to pay me as a consultant or give me equity as an advisor."

This made me rethink how I responded to the endless requests for my advice. I decided that I'd do a thirty-minute call or introductory meeting with a founder before requiring compensation as an official advisor. But I never would have known to ask for what I'm worth if my friend hadn't been transparent with me about how she handled her own consulting fee. Now, I make sure to stay on top of my current value and how it may change over time. When I'm having casual networking meetings with other advisors, I ask them, "What kind of equity have you been getting in the companies you advise?"

If you're not sure what you're worth, make an effort to find out. Services like Glassdoor have a lot of valuable salary information that you can look at to get a sense of what your peers are making. The recruiters you connect with can also tell you what type of compensation they're seeing based on your experience and career level.

Know All the Levers

I find that in negotiations we often narrowly define "compensation." When exploring a new job and thinking about the negotiation process, try to think more broadly. There's more to a compensation package than just a salary and benefits (though, of course, those are important). There are also often overlooked "perks" you can push for if the company is not willing to go higher on your salary.

Here are just a few:

- Flexible schedule (part-time or working remotely)
- Educational support (tuition reimbursement for continuing education or graduate courses)
- Bonuses
- Stock options

- Extra vacation time
- Gym membership
- Fridays off during the summer

Remember, too, that your priorities will shift over time. When I was in my twenties, salary was hugely important to me so my husband and I could start saving. By the time I was in my forties, flexibility became more important because of my children. Your priorities may be different than mine.

A friend of mine had a side hustle she was passionate about, and it was important to her that she was able to continue working on it. She was willing to forego a little on her full-time salary to have permission and flexibility to continue working on her side project. These are all pieces of the puzzle, and the importance of each will likely change over the course of your career. Decide which is most valuable for you *before* you begin a negotiation.

Time It Right

Your empathy is a great asset when determining the right moment to ask for what you deserve. When will your boss feel the most open and accepting of the discussion? I once had a boss who was like two different people in the morning and in the afternoon. Whenever I wanted something, I made sure to get time on his calendar early in the day to have the best chance of success. To me, this is the epitome of being empathetic *and* strategic.

No matter who your boss is, it's always a good time to ask if you've recently had a big, high-profile win at work. People in the company will know about your accomplishment, and your boss is not going to want to lose you. This is a time when you shouldn't wait for an annual review to ask for the raise or promotion you deserve. Instead, seize the moment when you have a lot of momentum and power.

Get the Data

Negotiations should always be more objective than subjective. By that I mean never let negotiations be about personal issues or what you "feel" you deserve. Along those lines, try to avoid talking about personal circumstances like expenses that you have to pay. Promotions and raises should be about performance and hard data, not feelings and extenuating circumstances. Those concerns are pretty much irrelevant to the company and can be easily swatted away.

Especially when you're feeling insecure in a negotiation, it's always a good idea to fall back on solid evidence you've collected to help you make your case. This can be data about your accomplishments or about the company's current financial picture. For example, prepare concrete evidence of the value you've created for your organization, whether you are a teacher who's launched a successful project at your school or an accountant who has implemented a program that saved the company a lot of money. Sometimes, the value you've added is not tied to a specific product or project. It may be that you've created a culture for your team that has resulted in improved morale and retention, or you took the initiative and launched a new business resource group at the company.

Financial data is just as important for you to have in mind when facing a negotiation. You have to have numbers at your fingertips to justify your requirements, including everything you may be leaving behind. For example, I recently mentored two different women who were both moving on from their jobs before the end of the year and would therefore be leaving their year-end bonuses on the table. Neither of them had thought to ask for a signing bonus with their new companies to compensate for that lost money. I explained that, from their new employers' perspectives, it would be difficult to argue with the hard data about the money they were leaving behind. And sure enough, both women were able to negotiate successfully for significant signing bonuses.

It's also hard to argue with market price. When I was at Time, Inc., a young woman on my team came to me and said, "Look, I know that people who are doing the same job as me at other media companies are making this much money. This is the range." She was right. And by presenting it to me in that way, she gave me no other option than to find a way to get her the raise she deserved — or risk losing her.

I've also relied on market data when negotiating in my own career. When I first took the job at Time, Inc., the title they offered me was general manager of *People* Digital. But I knew that the person who had the same position at *Sports Illustrated* had a president title. I went back to my future boss and asked for a title that matched, but he said, "*Sports Illustrated*'s digital brand is already a proven success. We're just getting *People* off the ground. How about we keep your title as GM and revisit it in a year when we see how we're doing?" I thought this was fair. After a year, we had proven success with the digital brand, and my boss was then comfortable giving me the president title.

When you're negotiating a salary, a promotion, or even a title, you might not get what you want right away. But if you get the data and ask, it's much more likely for you to end up on a path toward getting it.

Represent

Here's an intriguing fact. Research tells us that women actually outperform men when negotiating *on behalf of* someone else. Do women feel more comfortable when the negotiation is not about them because they don't risk coming across as greedy or because the person they're negotiating with doesn't penalize them because of these double standards? I would venture to say it's probably a little bit of both. This goes back to communal negotiations. Negotiating on behalf of someone else makes us seem like we care more about others than ourselves, a trait that's traditionally valued in women and reinforced by society.

To me, this is actually empowering. It shows that we do have the raw talent to do a good job of negotiating. But something happens when we're negotiating on behalf of ourselves—our confidence goes out the door. If this happens to you, the next time you're preparing to negotiate that salary increase or promotion, think about how you would approach the conversation *if you were representing your best friend or your sister instead of yourself.* Then, take that confidence and conviction and apply it to you!

What I Wish I Knew When I Asked for a Raise in My Twenties

When I was in my twenties, the thought of asking for a raise terrified me. *What if I get turned down? Will my boss think I'm greedy or pushy? Do I even really deserve more money?* This kind of hesitation holds many women back from asking for more at work. I get it, because I've been there—and I've mentored dozens of women who have been there, too. But while asking for a raise isn't always easy, I've learned that it certainly doesn't have to be terrifying, either. Below are five tips and reminders I wish I could tell my twenty-something self back when I was wondering whether (and how) to ask for more.

1. **Remember: the world is not going to end if you get "no" for an answer.** What's the worst thing that can happen after you ask for a raise? You're not going to get fired. You're not going to get a demotion. "No" obviously isn't the answer you want, but unless you're completely off base in your request, it won't damage your career or

cause anyone to see you in a negative light. If anything, it sends a message that you're confident, savvy, and serious about professional growth.

2. **You have succeeded before.** Keep a record of your accomplishments on an ongoing basis. Write them down, referencing specific numbers and examples whenever possible. When it's time to ask for a raise, these examples will remind you of why you deserve one. Better yet, they'll serve as proof points during your conversation. The most compelling requests for raises I've received focus on the person's impact and the concrete results she's achieved.

3. **Be confident and keep it positive.** The delivery of your message matters. If you sound like you're not sure about whether you deserve a raise, it may raise doubts for the person across the table. It will also tip them off that it's easy for them to say no. As such, be sure to maintain strong eye contact, sit up straight, and try to keep filler words like "um" and "just" to a bare minimum. Enter the meeting with high energy, being sure to emphasize what you love about your job and the company.

4. **Stop waiting for the perfect moment.** You can be strategic by using the timing tips earlier in this chapter. If you keep waiting for the perfect moment, however, you're going to be waiting a long time. There will always be a new potential accomplishment on the horizon. Don't procrastinate. Push yourself to ask now.

5. **Use "no" to fuel your next steps.** If your boss tells you it's not going to happen, ask why not. Get as much specific feedback as possible so you can figure out what steps you need to take to get to the next level. Leave the meeting knowing precisely what you have to accomplish and by when, and then check in regularly with your boss or manager to ensure you're on track.

On the Job Negotiations

We tend to think of negotiations in terms of salaries, promotions, and titles, but no matter what industry you're in, it's likely that you'll find yourself in some sort of negotiations while on the job, too. During the course of simply doing your job, you may end up negotiating for more resources (such as hiring more people on the team), contract terms with a vendor, a launch date for a specific initiative (which normally involves asking for more time), rates with a freelance worker, the overall budget for a certain project, and so on. The point is, learning how to become an effective negotiator is inevitably going to help you be better at your job.

Avoid Paying the A-Hole Tax

As intimidating as negotiating may seem, the truth is that being good at it relies on the very skills that "nice girls" tend to have in spades. Essentially, when you are authentically nice and use your empathy to build strong relationships, people are more likely to agree to favorable terms during a negotiation and say yes to your requests. Ann Frost, who teaches deal-making to executives, claims that when people are rude during negotiations, it ends up costing them. She calls this an "A-hole tax."

"Nobody likes to negotiate with an ass," she says, "so they make them pay an A-hole tax, often without even realizing it."

I have seen this happen in my own career. When I was at Moviefone, AOL acquired our company. I was running finance for Moviefone, so I was in charge of leading the due diligence on our side of the acquisition. Due diligence is a sticky process that can become confrontational because it involves setting a price for the company, and there's a lot at stake. I knew this going in and wanted to do whatever I could to avoid unproductive conflict.

I also knew that I'd be spending a lot of time with the people at AOL who were evaluating our business, so I made a big effort to get to know them on a personal level. At the same time, we had to convince the AOL folks that Moviefone was worth $525 million. It was a big responsibility to take them through the financials and explain our revenue models and assets, but I made sure to keep this process collaborative and inclusive and make it clear that we shared the same goal, which was for the deal to go through. We set up a conference room for the AOL team in our offices. Instead of sitting in my office all day, I spent a good part of my day sitting in the conference room doing my work while making myself available to the team if they had questions. By sharing space with them, I naturally got to know them on a personal level and developed relationships with the team.

This collaborative attitude paid off in so many ways after the acquisition was final. Now, we all had to work together, and I was starting off at an advantage because I had already developed positive relationships with the team. This made the transition much easier and smoother than it otherwise may have been.

I learned a lot from this experience and absolutely made sure to put relationships first at every stage of my career. Later, when I was at Time, Inc., Mitch Klaif was our chief information officer. As the head of technology, he was under a lot of pressure to keep the infrastructure running. I sensed that, in many ways, his was a thankless job. A lot of the people coming to him were unhappy—their email wasn't working or they didn't have the funding they needed for a project.

I took the time to get to know Mitch as a person, ask about his family, and listen when he was frustrated about something. So I got along with Mitch really well, while many of my colleagues had a hard time getting him to prioritize their initiatives. At one point, my team needed to accelerate a product launch, which meant we'd need a lot more resources from Mitch's team. I assumed my boss would ask him directly, but instead she said, "Fran, you need to ask Mitch. He can't say no to you."

Sure enough, when I walked into Mitch's office, he laughed and said, "Oh no, here she comes again. What are you going to get out of me this time, Fran?" When I got a yes from him (of course), my team was incredulous. But it wasn't magic. Mitch was inclined to say yes to me because we already had a relationship. In other words, I didn't just go to him when I had a problem or needed something. I connected with him on a personal level. This wasn't a power move. As a so-called "nice girl," being empathetic came naturally to me, and it simply worked to my advantage when it was time to negotiate or ask for something.

When They Go Low, "Nice Girls" Go High

Perhaps you're thinking, *"This is all fine and good, but what if the person you're negotiating with isn't as 'nice' as you are?"* Unfortunately, this happens far too often — a "nice girl" tries to use all of the kind and collaborative negotiating strategies in this chapter, but the person on the other side of the table isn't playing nice at all. Luckily, there are ways to successfully negotiate without ever stooping to a bully's level.

My friend Mimi Feliciano, a real estate expert and philanthropist, told me that she was trained in a technique called "Best Alternative to a Negotiated Agreement" (also known as "BATNA"), which helps you figure out what to do if a negotiation isn't working out. It often requires creative thinking to make a negotiation move forward collaboratively even when it starts to get ugly.

Mimi found that when she used this technique, she was able to find out-of-the-box, win-win solutions. For example, she was negotiating a big development deal that involved buying several different properties, and she needed one last piece to make it all work. But the owner was being a bully—mean, impossible, and unfair. Everything had to be his way. She had offered to split the difference between where she was and where he was, but he refused to budge.

Instead of becoming mad or defensive or stooping to the owner's level by pushing back on him to change his bottom line, Mimi became creative and thought about whether or not there was any other way to get the owner what he needed and still be whole (i.e., not lose money), so she looked to find an interested third party who might be able to help. She knew that the town where the development was located really wanted the project to go through. So she went to them and explained her dilemma, and they offered to mediate the agreement. With the town's assistance, the negotiation worked out so that everyone got something and the project moved forward.

A hard-line negotiator may have seen this as a failure because Mimi didn't get the owner to budge on his number. But looking at it through a more collaborative lens, it was a win for Mimi, the owner, and the town because they all ended up with what they wanted, and the project moved forward. Mimi's goal was not to beat the other person, but rather to collaborate with them so they could both win. And that's exactly what she did.

Empathy and Negotiation— A Win-Win

To me, a successful negotiation results in a win for both sides, not a situation where I've bulldozed the other side into giving me what I want at their expense. For both sides to win, they each need to truly understand what is important to the other. This requires real empathy.

I first learned this art of empathetic negotiation from my father. As a skilled worker, my father often had to negotiate his fee for a project. When we first moved to New York from Italy, his English wasn't very good, so he relied on nonverbal communication to express his confidence and authentic kindness. He held the other person's gaze, affectionately tapped them on the shoulder, and always smiled. He was charming. But his kindness was always grounded in an understanding of where the other person was coming from and what was important to them. My dad's entire business depended on word-of-mouth referrals, so he wanted everyone who left a negotiation with him to feel good about it.

While my dad did this intuitively—he was never formally trained to negotiate—experts agree that using empathy is the best way to get to a win-win outcome. Negotiation expert William Ury says that a successful negotiation is one that improves the relationship between the participants. To do this, instead of trying to maintain a winning position, you must focus on the interests of both parties—the things you are each trying to change, create, and/or protect. Once you're clear on your respective goals, you can find a way to both get what you want.

A woman I mentor named Anna recently took on a new role in marketing for a big newspaper publisher. Her first assignment was to find new software to manage their customer database. Anna found a startup with a really impressive product that she thought would work well for her company. When it came time to negotiate the monthly licensing fee, she wasn't sure what amount would be fair. She came to me asking for advice about how to negotiate the fee.

My response surprised Anna. I asked, "Why would you pay anything at all?" I told Anna that she was bringing so much value to this startup just by working with them because her employer was a major publisher. That is, it would be a huge coup for the startup to have a renowned company like that as their first partner. Based on my feedback, Anna decided to negotiate a free three-month pilot program with the startup.

I encouraged her to start by voicing what Anna thought the other party wanted, as well as her own goals. She could say, for example, "I imagine that your goal is to get your software into as many customers' hands as possible. Signing on with a major publisher will give you a lot of credibility that will be more valuable to you than a monthly licensing fee. My goal is for my company to find the most effective software to communicate with our customers with the least amount of financial risk possible. I'm sure that if we put our heads together, we can come up with a way to ensure both of our needs are met."

If the other party agreed about those goals, I told Anna to move onto the actual proposal: "So here's how I'm thinking about this. We can do a three-month pilot, during which I'm willing to invest resources in testing the software. You'll get to tell people that we're your first customer, and you'll get all of our feedback when the three months are up, which will make the product even stronger. This way, we'll get to try out the product without taking a risk, and if it works out after the three months, we can start paying a licensing fee."

Finally, I told Anna that if she got stuck to keep coming back to, "How can we make this work?" By saying "we," she would nicely and empathetically remind the other person that they were on the same team. Instead of competing, they were in this together. As it developed, this type of negotiation came naturally to Anna, and she came to terms with the startup founder that ended up being a win for both of them.

Key Takeaways

- Women don't tend to negotiate for themselves as much as their male peers. This is a major factor in the gender wage gap. Instead of accepting a first offer, never be afraid to ask for what you deserve.

- In negotiations, focus on the objective and true value you add to the organization instead of all the reasons you feel you want a higher salary. Gather as much data as possible ahead of time to use as backup.
- Empathy is an asset when negotiating on the job. Always try to link what you want with what the other party wants, and if you get stuck, go back to, "How can we make this work?"
- It often takes creative problem solving to find a solution when facing a tough negotiation. When this happens, ask yourself, "What is the best alternative to a negotiated agreement?"

7

Invest in Yourself *and*
Be a Team Player

ABOUT EIGHT YEARS AGO, I HEARD PAT FILI-
Krushel, a senior executive at Time Warner, talking about how she
routinely went to two or three networking meetings a day. This absolutely shocked me! I couldn't imagine how she found the time
for that kind of schedule. But Pat continued to explain that as she
looked back over the course of her career, the one factor that she
felt aided her success more than anything else was the incredible
network she had built over time. She felt strongly that her connections had helped her get from one job to another.

Well, okay, I thought. *This is important.* At the time, I didn't
know what my next gig was going to be. I had been working in digital media for over ten years, and I realized that I needed to broaden
my horizons to meet people outside of digital—people who didn't
necessarily look or think like me, who could show me what other
possibilities might be out there. I thought if Pat could do two or
three networking meetings a day, then I ought to be able to do at
least one coffee a day. That was the beginning of the journey that
led to a whole new career.

The first thing I did was reconnect with Patricia Karpas, who
you read about earlier—the dear friend I'd worked with at AOL

years before. As it turned out, she was working on a variety of nonprofit initiatives and had even adopted an orphanage in Africa. At the time, I was doing very little on the nonprofit side, and meeting with her inspired me to start doing more.

That connection led me to meet more people in the nonprofit space, and eventually, to read the book, *Half the Sky* by Nicholas Kristof and Sheryl WuDunn, about the oppression of women around the world. The book got me thinking about what I wanted to give back to the world. What was I truly passionate about?

At the end of the book, the authors include a list of resources for people who want to take action to make a difference. One of these was the nonprofit organization GlobalGiving. After researching GlobalGiving online, I was so impressed with what they were doing that I tracked down and emailed the CEO, Mari Kuraishi. I wrote, "Hi, I'm Fran, and I work at *People*. I love what you are doing and would love to be helpful to you." When we met, I explained that, for years, I had been using digital to entertain people —at Moviefone, AOL, and *People*—and now I was interested in using the same digital medium in a more impactful way. This was exactly what GlobalGiving was doing.

I asked Mari what the organization's biggest challenges were and how I might be helpful based on my knowledge and experience. She immediately said, "We're a D.C.-based organization, and I would love your help expanding our support base in New York." Together, we came up with the idea of creating a New York Leadership Council for GlobalGiving, which I cofounded with Brian Walsh, whom Mari later introduced me to.

This was eight years ago, and I've been working with GlobalGiving ever since. I'm currently on their board and have served as the board chair. This path was all set in motion simply because I decided to reconnect with Patricia.

With my new commitment to networking, I also began meeting people in the tech startup world. Knowing that I had always been passionate about mentoring young women, my friend Greg Clayman told me, "You need to meet Soraya Darabi. She was at the *New York Times* doing social media. Now she's doing a startup. She's a force. At twenty-six, she was on the cover of *Fast Company* as one of the most creative people in business."

When I met Soraya, we hit it off right away. One day she said to me, "I know all these female founders who are having such a hard time getting access to financial resources and mentorship. You would be amazing at helping with that."

My gut told me that Soraya was right. Pivoting to investing would give me a tremendous amount of flexibility, which I welcomed given that I had two toddlers at the time. It would also allow me to do more mentoring while also learning about a whole new industry. And as I had already been spending so much of my time giving free advice to startup founders anyway, investing in them made a lot of sense. That's the short story of how I went from media to investing. Since then, I have built a portfolio of nineteen companies, sixteen of which are female-founded.

Here's my overall point: there is no way I would be where I am today if I hadn't begun to grow my network as Pat suggested all those years ago. The story of how I got from there to here is a perfect example of what can happen when we focus on connecting with others outside the office.

Before being inspired to really grow my network, I had kept my head down and focused mostly on contributing to the company. I'm not the only one. In Chapter 2, I discussed the messaging we receive beginning at a young age, telling us to be "good girls" who sit at our desks and get our jobs done. As a result, many of the "nice girls" I mentor feel an obligation to "do the right thing" and do right by the company and team. To them, this means working as hard as they can and spending as much time as possible in the office. They spend their time taking on additional tasks, fixing problems that nobody else wants to deal with, and staying at the office late and coming in early. As I said earlier, there's nothing wrong with going the extra mile like this, but it *does* become a problem if it leaves you with no time left over to focus on developing yourself and your own career. That's not being nice; that's being a people pleaser.

Of course you have to do your job and do it well, but you actually have to do even more than that to succeed. You also need to proactively reach out to people whom you don't work with on a daily basis. Without those key contacts, it's easy to become isolated in a situation where the very people who can help you get ahead — and who you can be the most helpful to — have no idea how good you are, what your true interests are, or, for that matter, that you even exist.

I've seen so many "nice girls" who felt obligated to keep their heads down all day end up getting stuck at dead-end jobs or worse — desperate when their jobs go away. In other words, many women feel pressured to focus on the group (team or organization) instead of the self (professional and personal development). This pressure was echoed in the following statements from the women I surveyed:

- "Whenever I leave the office for a meeting, I feel guilty, as if my colleagues will think I'm being lazy or slacking off. I already get dirty looks when I leave the office at five to pick up my kids, and this makes it even worse."
- "I told my boss that I wanted to take a public speaking course, but he said no because it wasn't directly related to my current role. But how am I supposed to grow into a new role one day if I don't develop my skills?"
- "I love the idea of networking more, but I just don't have time. I'm already working eighty hours a week. When could I possibly fit this in?"

I used to feel this way, too. But I've learned throughout my career that it *is* possible to be a team player while still keeping your head up and growing yourself professionally, networking with others, and thinking about your future. And finding time to focus on your career doesn't mean you're doing the wrong thing or betraying your employer! The things you learn from others while you're out networking can benefit you *and* your company. Even better, the very qualities that make you nice will work to your advantage once you commit to getting up from your desk and engaging with the wider world around you. My own experiences can attest to the fact that once you do, people will want to help you, work with you, and support your development.

There are three things that we should all be doing to stay relevant throughout our work lives and strike that perfect balance between being a "nice" team player and focusing on our careers:

- Invest in yourself
- Build your network
- Connect the dots

Invest in Yourself

To invest in yourself and your future, you must build relationships within your company, do extracurricular activities that may plant future seeds, and stay on top of industry trends.

Build Relationships Within Your Company

Every coffee break and lunch ought to be a chance to meet people, share ideas, forge new bonds, and solidify relationships. Avoid the impulse to sit at your desk all day to get work done. Meeting your colleagues is how you'll learn if there is another area in the company you may want to move into. Plus, networking with others who can help you get things done more efficiently is good for you *and* for the company.

Most large companies have business resource groups that are

organized around gender, function, ethnicity, or sexual orientation. When you find yourself in a business meeting that includes multiple departments, avoid the inclination to sit next to someone you already know. If there is someone in the meeting who is working on an interesting project, ask him or her to coffee. When there is a cross-functional project, offer to help. Getting access to a different part of the company may open your eyes to a position or career you never thought of pursuing. At the very least, it will help you do your job more effectively because you'll have established relationships with colleagues in other departments.

Do Extracurricular Activities That May Plant Future Seeds

Pursue other interests outside of your job. Volunteer. Join an industry association. The more you follow your passions, the more you can plant seeds for your future. During my tenure at Time, Inc., I joined nonprofit boards and dipped my toe into startup investing. I was following my interests, but I was also planting seeds. In fact, I'm still planting seeds today. While investing in and advising startups is my main job, I'm also writing this book and advising the TV show *Girl Starter*. It's the next step in the evolution of my interest in mentoring and investing in women. If you broaden your horizons through activities outside of the office, you may end up falling in love with one of these areas and making it your next chapter.

Stay on Top of Industry Trends

One of the most important things you can do is to pay attention to cultural forces and industry trends. There are two crucial reasons to do this.

First, if you see a trend that could be a revenue opportunity for your company—maybe it's a new consumer behavior or emerging technology—raise your hand to lead a team that will pursue it. As you read in Chapter 2, this is a great way to create an opportunity for yourself and your company.

If you haven't been at the company for long enough and/or lack the political capital or credibility to get something started, this may mean that you have to do the work to prove that there is an opportunity here. Maybe you can start by chatting with a peer at another company that is dabbling in the space and finding out what their early results are.

Second, it's important to study industry trends so that you stay relevant. A woman I mentored named Alicia had been working at a small ad agency for ten years when she met me. She had started out as an assistant to one of the partners and worked her way up to running a creative team. Then, the partners decided to sell the company to a larger firm (part of the consolidation in the industry that so much of advertising has gone through as the landscape has changed to digital).

Alicia didn't like the new owners and didn't have the digital experience they favored. When she thought about leaving, however, she didn't even know where to start. Her days had consisted of answering emails and sitting in meetings. Because she loved what she was doing, she hadn't taken calls from recruiters or bothered to keep up with the digital transformation in the industry. Now she was panicking.

To avoid ending up like Alicia, it's essential to keep up with what's going on within your industry. Many of us feel disloyal or selfish for thinking ahead, but the hard truth is that no company is going to be that devoted to you in return. You must put your own career first.

Build Your Network

In the years since I saw Pat speak at Time Warner, I've seen how networking has been a critical skill for my professional and personal success. Yes, it can be intimidating and it takes time, but it truly matters. It's the most effective way to find people and opportunities that can help you advance, develop your career, and find new avenues for development and fulfillment. And it can help you whether or not you want to leave your organization.

I've met many "nice girls" who feel uncomfortable with the concept of networking. Some mentees of mine have described it as feeling "use-y," like you're socializing with an agenda to take advantage of the other person, and that doesn't feel authentic or comfortable to them.

If you feel ambivalent about networking, remember that you're not using anyone or serving yourself when you meet people. Networking is a two-way street, or, more accurately, as the word suggests, it's about creating a web of connections—ones that can help you and can help the other people in the network, too.

Janet Comenos, the CEO of the startup Spotted Media, recently shared with me a great example of how helping someone else ultimately aided her. It's the quintessential story of how "nice girls" can and often do finish first. She was attending a networking event and feeling guilty because she was really supposed to be preparing a fundraising pitch deck. (Sound familiar?) She noticed a young man in the corner whom no one was talking to, so Janet went over just to be nice. It turned out he was looking for help in sales, which was her area of expertise. He asked if she would come to his office to talk to his team. Despite being so busy, she said yes and spent two and a half hours with his team.

Janet was happy to do this because so many people had been generous with her as she started her company that she made this kind of activity a priority. And this favor turned out to be beneficial to Janet, too. The young man was so grateful that he made introductions on her behalf to both the firm that is building the platform for Janet's company and to the person who ended up being her lead investor in her current fundraising round. That's a perfect example of how networking has the power to benefit all parties involved—and, of course, it shows the power of authentic kindness!

How to Get Your Name Out to Executive Recruiters

Relationships with recruiters can help you find jobs, negotiate higher salaries based on market data they provide, and even pinpoint opportunities that you may have never considered. But how can you connect with them?

Actually, it's not as difficult as you may think. Remember, recruiters' jobs depend on their own networks, so they are always hungry to meet more people. Here are three very simple ways of developing these relationships:

1. Research the top recruiters in your field and ask to be introduced to them by mutual connections on LinkedIn.
2. Find out who the top recruiters are in your field by asking your friends and peers. Every time you have lunch or coffee with a colleague, ask, "I'm interested in developing relationships with recruiters. Do you know anyone good who you'd recommend?"
3. Attend relevant conferences in your industry. This is where recruiters often go to scout for talent.

Network Intentionally

When you do network, there are specific things you can do to make sure you are doing it as effectively as possible.

Don't Be Afraid to Ask

In a recent survey of men and women, researchers discovered that women in general have a less goal-oriented approach to networking. They focus on finding common ground and socializing, while men have no problem approaching someone and bluntly stating what they want.

"Men generally go into networking opportunities with more clarity of what they want to achieve and focus solely on their professional needs," notes Cathy Goddard of Lighthouse Visionary Strategies, who has run networking groups for many years. "Women often take a selfless approach and are more apt to consider what they have to give others. They hesitate to ask for what they want, whereas men are more comfortable making direct demands."

Thinking of others isn't a problem as long as you don't fall into the trap of giving and never asking for anything in return from the people you're networking with. Remember, that two-way networking street goes in your direction, too! Make sure you're being clear about your aspirations and "asks" in addition to what value you can provide.

For example, at every single meeting I've attended lately, I ask, "As I transition to creating a marketing plan for my book, I'd love to come back to you and ask for your support." I often tailor this to whomever I'm speaking to. If they work for a big company, I say, "I'd love to come speak at your company about the book when it comes out." If I'm talking to a reporter, I say, "I would love it if you'd cover the book." So many of these people have responded positively with their own ideas about how they can be helpful—but they probably wouldn't have thought to do this if I hadn't initially been specific about my asks.

Diversify Your Network
Both men and women tend to build networks comprised of people of their own gender. We gravitate toward people like us. This is a universal tendency, but you will probably miss a lot of opportunities by failing to extend your connections all the way up to the peo-

ple at the top, who still often tend to be men. New research published in the *Harvard Business Review* suggests that one of the reasons fewer women reach the top of the corporate ladder than men is that they are less likely to hear about available positions as early as their male counterparts.

"Men tend to be in the top positions in organizations so, structurally, they're in a position to hear about job openings or opportunities when they arrive, and circulate those to their networks," said Lisa Torres, a George Washington University sociology professor who studies the hiring and job-search process in corporations. In other words, men pass job openings to their mostly-male networks, and so the news reaches women only after it has passed through several men.

To level the playing field, we must add more men—especially high-status men—to our networks and make our interests and competencies crystal clear so that these men think of us first when an opportunity arises. How many men are in your network? Who can help you connect to some more, especially those who can help you advance?

Some of the most important mentors in my life have been men, from Lamar Chesney at Coke to Adam Slutsky at Moviefone and Paul Caine and David Geithner at Time, Inc. Lamar took a chance on me and promoted me into a job that, on paper, I was nowhere near ready for. Adam encouraged me to transition to digital media. Paul and David were powerhouses at Time and very connected to the CEO and other officers at the company. They were among the first to learn about reorganizations and new opportunities and, being champions of mine, I certainly benefited from that early knowledge.

Of course, I'm not suggesting that you ignore your fellow women as you rise to the top. One of my biggest priorities has been to pull women into my network and to advocate for them. If enough of us do this, it will go a long way toward balancing the ratio of men and women in leadership positions.

Put Networking into Action

To give you a sense of how to get up from your desk and into action, let's return to Alicia. As you read earlier, she found herself in a sticky situation, with few connections and what was looking like a dead-end job at an advertising firm that had been recently acquired. She came to me looking for help finding a new role. Here are the three steps she took to start networking:

Step 1: Create a Networking Strategy

First, we talked about two kinds of networking—*open-ended networking* and *purposeful networking*. Open-ended networking is about *building your web* of connections, while purposeful networking is *identifying that individual* within your web of connections who can help you get what you need. You need to do both kinds of networking in order to get ahead. However, it's nearly impossible to target one specific person for purposeful networking if you don't already have a network in which to find him or her!

I asked Alicia to think about the people she knew whose work she admired. While Alicia didn't have a big network, she did have some connections—she just needed to figure out who they were and begin reaching out to them. She started by creating a mind map, drawing the connections she had and all the other people they were connected to.

Alicia's mind map gave her a place to begin. Then, the power of a "warm introduction"—an introduction by a mutual acquaintance—allowed her to go from one person on that map to another. For busy people, a warm intro is a kind of shorthand for trust. If you are introduced by a mutual acquaintance, that person has in some way vouched for you. Rarely will you get a response to a "cold" email; likewise, rarely will you be ignored if you've received a warm intro.

If you're wondering how to ask someone to make an introduction for you, here's an example of an email I received recently from a young woman that I thought was particularly well worded and effective:

"Hello Fran, I hope this email finds you well. I wanted to reach out because I'm very interested in applying to the JOB TITLE with COMPANY NAME. I noticed that you're connected with NAME at the company. I am wondering if you know her well enough to potentially pass along my name and resume to her. I know that networking is a very important step in the job application process, and I would really appreciate it if you have the ability to help me make this connection."

I wrote back, "Can you please send me a forwardable email with resume attached? Happy to send along!" And, just like that, this young woman received a warm introduction to a powerful person at her dream company.

After you've created a mind map and strategy, then you need to set your networking goals. What types of people do you want to meet and to what end? How often are you going to get "out there"? And finally, how much of your networking will be technology-assisted and how much will be good old-fashioned face-to-face networking?

When Alicia decided to make networking her priority, she decided her goals were to meet established advertising professionals who could potentially become mentors and refer her to opportunities and get her name out in the advertising world as someone worth knowing, and ideally, hiring. She decided to tell Tom, the partner she had been the closest to at her company, that she was looking to move on. (He'd already taken a package and had left the company.)

Alicia asked Tom not only to personally connect her to industry heavyweights, but also to invite her to industry events that might be "punching above her weight." This took some courage, but Tom had great respect for Alicia from the ten years she had worked for him, and that made him more than happy to say yes. Tom had a huge network and was tied to all sorts of movers and shakers in his industry.

But Alicia couldn't just rely on Tom's connections. She needed to expand her own connections by figuring out where else to network. Technology platforms like LinkedIn and industry-specific online communities can—and should—be a big part of your networking strategy. So should conferences, industry mixers, and meet-ups. Subscribe to email lists and online groups related to the industry you are interested in. Many conferences and events have their own social networking groups as well. Sign up for all of these, pay attention, and participate.

True, not all industries have frequent conferences or meet-ups. You may need to work harder to find opportunities to "show up." Attend lectures, read books, and seek out opportunities to connect with people in person. You can also consider creating your own networking group. I told Alicia about a woman I knew who had organized two different groups to meet with similarly ambitious young women. In one group, talking about anything not work-related is off limits. In the other, which she calls her "lean back" circle, work talk is off limits. Alicia loved that idea and started two groups of her own.

In addition, Alicia found several networking groups focused on her industry, including Advertising Women of New York, and began to attend their functions. Once she had a sense of whom she wanted to meet and Tom and others started making warm introductions for her, she had to set some discipline around making enough time to network. She knew it had to be a priority or she wouldn't do it. Because she was playing catch-up and time was of the essence, she decided to commit to one hour of networking a day.

Step 2: Show Up

Showing up means being physically present (or virtually present when you're networking online), but it also means so much more than that. If you go to a networking event and stand in the corner staring into your drink, no one will notice you. Worse, they might notice you and form a negative impression. If you're shy, it takes a lot of courage to put yourself into a situation where you show up with confidence and make your presence known. You may be surprised to hear that I'm actually an introvert myself, so I know how hard this can be.

Alicia decided not to go to events with a friend because she knew she'd end up talking only to her friend and not meeting anyone new. She followed some tips for icebreakers that I gave her (below) and prepared her talking points in advance. And because she knew it would be easy for her to be helpful to others and forget about her own agenda, she made a commitment to herself to be sure to be explicit about what she was looking for—a new opportunity in advertising—with every person she spoke to.

Top Tips for Introductions and Icebreakers

I know how intimidating it can be to walk into an event and to start introducing yourself to perfect strangers. It can be even more difficult to talk about yourself without feeling like you're bragging or acting pushy. It has been important for me to develop specific strategies to introduce myself and break the ice without feeling inauthentic. Here are my top tips:

Make the Conversation About Them

This strategy works especially well for "nice girls" who are genuinely curious about the people they're meeting and don't want to feel like they're bragging. It's also extremely helpful if you're shy. All you need to do is formulate an initial question or comment and then let the other person do the talking. If possible, do your research ahead of time and see who's attending a particular event that you'd like to network with. Then try one of the following openers:

- "I read that you're working on X. That's so exciting; I'd love to hear more about it."
- "I've been following your career and am a big fan."
- "What are you working on that you're excited about these days?"
- "The last time we saw each other, you were working on X. What ever happened with that?"

This strategy still works well if you don't know anyone at the event. In this case, tweak your opening question accordingly:

- "How do you know the host?"
- "What brings you here?"
- "Is this your first time attending one of these events?"

Find Common Ground

If you do your research beforehand—and you should—it's very likely that you'll find you have something in common with the people you are looking to develop connections with. If so, that makes a great opener. Try one of these:

- "I see that we both know Sally Smith. Isn't she great? How do you know her?"
- "I noticed on LinkedIn that we went to the same college! What was your experience like there?"
- "I see that we both work in digital media. What current trends are you most excited about?"

Get Introduced

If you know the host or someone else attending an event, ask her, "Who do you think I should make sure to connect with?" Chances are, she'll offer to introduce you to a few people. If not, why not ask for that, too? If she suggests that you meet someone in particular, you can respond by saying, "That's a great idea, thanks. Would you mind introducing me to her?" An in-person introduction is just as valuable as a warm email introduction (if not more so).

If you're networking online, showing up means not just reading online forums, but also commenting and engaging. You need to follow people on Twitter, retweet them, interact with them, and comment on their blogs. Use your authentic niceness to really connect. My friend Tereza Nemessanyi, Microsoft's Entrepreneur-in-Residence, made her way into the tech scene from a career in management consulting with a strategy she called, "A Hundred Events, a Thousand Comments."

Tereza immersed herself in the online life of the industry she wanted to be part of. As she got to know the players and the themes, she began to comment on blogs, setting herself a personal goal of making a thousand comments, a number she felt would be enough to make her known within that community. She also set a goal of attending a hundred industry events during the same time period. These included meet-ups, pitch events, and even a conference that normally cost thousands a ticket, but she called the organizers to see if she could attend for free if she volunteered to work a couple of hours at the conference. Pretty quickly, all of those events led to lots of coffee dates, which she included in the hundred events needed to get to her goal. Her current role at Microsoft shows that her strategy clearly worked!

Of course, there are many other ways to make a great first impression. Not long ago, I delivered an address at a big conference. After my talk, I was swamped with people who wanted to meet me. But there was one woman who stood out. She had a big smile on her face, a great presence, and a confident energy. And she was carrying a gift bag. "Hi Fran, I'm Lisa Mayer from My Social Canvas," she said as she reached out to shake my hand. "I know how committed you are to causes that support young women and girls. I'm working on something I'm really excited about that I would love to share with you." Then she handed me the gift bag.

Lisa and I had been introduced via email previously, but I'd been too busy to meet with her in person. As I found out more, I was excited about what she was working on. The gift was an example of the kind of work her company did. She needed a nonprofit partner that also focused on women's issues, so I introduced her to Dayle Haddon of WomenOne.

Together, they have since developed a Project Runway-style competition for Lisa's My Social Canvas designers. #Design4Her-Education, as the initiative came to be known, featured celebrity judges including supermodel Christy Turlington, actress Kelly Rutherford, and fashion designer Catherine Malandrino. Lisa used her niceness to show up in a big way that caught my attention and paid off for her business.

Like Lisa, you need to show up every day—at work, at parties, at coffee dates, at your volunteer positions—with confidence, putting your best face forward, being willing to meet new people, to introduce yourself, to say why you are there. Showing up is about having presence and speaking up on your own behalf.

Are you too shy? Not sure what to say? Not sure you could be as gutsy as Lisa was when introducing yourself to a new contact? Try role-playing with a friend, practicing in front of the mirror, or even attending a public speaking course to improve your networking skills.

Step 3: Make Personal Connections

As well as getting my attention with her charisma and kindness, Lisa had managed to figure out that I would be the exact right person for her to approach. No amount of gift bags would have worked if I hadn't been interested in what she was doing. But she had a plan to connect with me. You can and should make a similar plan when you are in "purposeful" networking mode.

Notice that Lisa had done research on me and knew the issues I was passionate about. Background research is crucial. Alicia did the same thing in pursuing an advertising position. Once her former boss made warm introductions for her, she spent time online researching each person and thinking about how she could provide real value to him or her.

Before you arrive at any networking event, read the industry trade news beforehand. Better still, read the trades on a regular basis. Be prepared to discuss the news or ask a question about what you've read. If you're meeting with a specific person, be sure to have checked their Twitter, LinkedIn, and blogs beforehand. This kind of preparation will give you confidence going into a meeting.

If you still feel uncomfortable making an ask when networking, lead with a kind offer. When I'm networking, I always try to glean if I can be helpful in any way. If I'm in a one-on-one situation with someone new, I might ask directly, "Is there some way I might be able to help?" In more casual meetings and at larger events, I'll only ask if it feels appropriate. Being able to be helpful in some way isn't about being a people pleaser; it gives me an opportunity to reach back out to them later in a way that feels more authentic. Even if nothing profound comes out of a first connection, I'm still building a valuable web.

After following all of these tips for several months, Alicia ended up meeting a woman who had just started an ad agency and was impressed by Alicia's experience in building creative teams. She invited Alicia to join her. And while she now loves what she's doing, Alicia has also learned her lesson. She continues to attend networking events and grow her network so that she never has to feel out on a limb when the winds of change blow again.

Connect the Dots

Career success is increasingly defined not just by how many hours you spend at your computer, but also by your ability to connect to others, incorporate outside perspectives, and navigate groups. These are essential skills in today's ultra-connected world because no one and nothing exists in a vacuum. This means connecting the dots among ideas, businesses, and people. You connect the dots when you pair all of the things you've learned when investing in yourself with your amazing network. For example, you spot a new trend and then tap into your network to find a partner to create a new product with you.

As a "nice girl," you have an advantage here *as long as you get up from your desk*, because a lot of this connecting requires the very same people skills that you have spent a lifetime developing. But if you aren't investing in yourself and networking, you won't be having the experiences and insights that will lead to connecting the dots.

I owe my entire career in digital to being able to successfully connect the dots. I was the director of finance for Coke's New York division in 1998. I was thirty and running a team of over one hundred people for one of the world's most admired companies. I wasn't thinking about leaving. But one day, I got a call from an executive recruiter about a senior vice president of finance role at Moviefone. I didn't know what Moviefone was, but subsequently learned it was a phone-based movie show times and ticketing service (aka 1-800-777-FILM).

In my discussions with the recruiter, what interested me most was how Moviefone was planning to expand to the internet. It would be the first company to provide movie show times and ticketing online. This was the late nineties, when consumers were starting to move to the internet for activities like shopping and entertainment, and I saw an exciting opportunity. So I agreed to take a meeting with Adam Slutsky, the COO and cofounder of Movie-fone. I liked him immediately and felt that I could learn a lot from him about the online space. I could tell that this new role would give me a chance to try something more entrepreneurial outside of my current realm of finance.

Switching from finance to marketing would have been very difficult—if not impossible—within a large corporation like Coke. There is much more flexibility at an early stage company. My colleagues at Coke thought I was crazy to leave a company that was so stable, but I'm so glad I made the leap because it led me to an entirely new career in digital. Looking back, I can see that I was able to spot that opportunity, fundamentally, because I picked my head up from my desk to network with recruiters and focus on industry trends—and then connect the dots between them.

Later, when I was at Time, Inc., I told my team to come to me if there was an opportunity that we should be capitalizing on or a major obstacle we needed to overcome. Whenever they showed up at my door, one of my first questions always was: "*Have you talked to people outside our company?*" You don't need to reinvent the wheel. What are other companies' best practices? What are they doing in this space? Don't feel guilty or disloyal for spending time outside of the office.

Remember, you're doing your company a service by bringing them all of this information. Go to conferences, meet people for coffee, come back with fresh ideas, and add even more value because you've invested in yourself, networked, and then connected the dots!

Key Takeaways

- You must find time to invest in yourself and your career. This isn't selfish—it will also be good for the company you work for because you'll add extra value.

- Plant seeds for your future by pursuing an interest or hobby outside of work.
- When networking, while it's great to focus on relationships, try to balance this by being clear on what your "asks" are.
- Commit to scheduling regular networking coffee, lunch, or drinks. Yes, this does take time, but it's essential.
- Connect the dots by pairing the skills and information you learn while investing in yourself with people in your network.

8

Set Boundaries *and* Be Caring

WHEN I WAS WORKING AT COKE, ANY TIME A last-minute task or request came up, I was the first person to raise my hand and volunteer to stay late and do it. At the time, I thought this was purely a good thing because it showed that I was ambitious and dedicated to the company. And for the most part, it *was* a good thing. Stepping up like that certainly helped me get noticed, but in doing so, I was unaware of the expectations I was creating by always offering to take on last-minute requests.

One evening, at about 5 p.m., I was in a meeting with the entire department. My boss had just gotten a directive from the CEO for our team to put together a report that night; he needed it first thing in the morning. This time, instead of asking for a volunteer, my boss just turned to me and asked, "Fran, can you stay late tonight and get the report done?" For a moment, I was flummoxed and unsure of how to respond. I suddenly understood I had been *too* accommodating. By consistently being eager to take on more, I had set a precedent, and now my boss expected me to *always* be available.

I stayed late and got the report done. It wasn't the end of the world, but I couldn't help but feel a little resentful about the situation. Plus, I was concerned about how to handle this situation the next time it happened, as I knew it inevitably would. At something of a loss, I reached out to a mentor in another department at the company and explained my dilemma. Without hesitation, she said, "Fran, you need to create boundaries, or people will keep taking advantage of you."

This was the first time I'd heard the word "boundaries" in a work setting. I explained to my mentor that I wanted to be considerate and helpful and make sure I never came across as lazy or uncooperative. She responded, "I understand that, but if you don't draw a line in the sand, people will walk all over you. Plus, all of your peers are seeing this. If you don't stand up for yourself, they'll think they can take advantage of you, too."

I'd love to say that the next time my boss asked me to complete a last-minute work assignment, I stood firm and asserted my boundaries. But in truth, it took a few more times for me to decide that I'd had enough. He called me into his office and asked me to stay late one night to write another report. I had practiced what I was going to say in such a situation with my mentor, so I was prepared to respond nicely but firmly while injecting a little humor to lighten a potentially uncomfortable conversation. I said:

"I've been struggling with how to talk to you about this. Over the past two weeks I've had to change my personal plans three times at the last minute to stay late. I'm afraid my boyfriend is going to break up with me! But truthfully, I wonder if this is a good opportunity for someone else on the team to step up and pitch in."

My boss was taken aback at first. Then he said, "I'm sorry, Fran, I just assumed. You always volunteer for these things, and I guess I just got used to asking you."

I already knew I was complicit in creating this dynamic, but it wasn't until the next week when another last-minute task came up that I fully understood how complex this situation really was. This time, my boss gathered the team in the conference room again and asked my colleague Josh to stay late to work on the project. Part of me was relieved, but I admit there was a small part of me that felt overlooked. I automatically feared I was missing out on an opportunity. Be careful what you wish for, right?

In the end, I swallowed that doubt and reminded myself to have confidence in my contributions. There would be plenty more opportunities to take on extra work; I didn't have to be the one to do it every single time in order to prove my worth. Going forward, my boss was better about spreading these assignments around, and I gradually gained confidence in asserting my boundaries.

I am not trying to discourage you from stepping up and volunteering to take on responsibilities, especially early on in your career when you want to make a good impression. But it is important to look at how you're being treated compared to your peers. If you're being asked to "pitch in" or "do a favor" more often than they are, you want to make sure you're not being taken advantage of.

It's also critically important to create boundaries at work to help you cut out extraneous tasks so you can focus on the things that matter. Without clear-cut boundaries, it's so easy to get caught up in the minutiae and let the important things slide, especially if you're a "nice girl" who wants to please others by never saying no.

Of course, this isn't a problem that's exclusive to our professional lives. Between our inclination to prioritize relationships and the threat of being perceived as selfish or bitchy for saying no, setting boundaries and sticking to them—and doing so nicely—can be incredibly difficult. Here's what some of the women I surveyed had to say:

- "I find it really difficult to say no to people, but then I get stressed and overwhelmed and can't follow through on all my commitments."

- "I keep strict boundaries between my work and personal lives, but I worry that this hurts me because people think I'm unfriendly or a bitch."
- "I'm so busy completing boring, administrative tasks that I can never seem to find time to focus on big, important projects. How can I balance this?"

The Four Square Model for Setting Boundaries

After my experience at Coke, I gradually got better at setting boundaries at work and maintaining them. But this is something I've never stopped learning, and many years later, my boundaries were challenged again in a big way.

I was just a few weeks into my maternity leave after adopting my second son when I heard that the company had just named a new CEO. Several of my colleagues emailed me saying, "You'd better get in here; she's developing relationships with the key people, and you're missing out."

Anxious and fearful of missing out on making a connection with the new CEO, I cut my maternity leave short and went back to work. But in retrospect, I saw that this wasn't necessary or particularly strategic. I could have reached out to the CEO and asked to meet for lunch to make a connection and then continued my leave. Instead, I allowed my aversion to saying no to take over my decision, and my boundaries came crashing down.

Now I was back at work at my demanding job, plus I had an eighteen-month-old and a newborn at home. I was so overwhelmed that I went into what I call "transactional mode." I so badly wanted to feel accomplished by checking things off my to-do list that I spent all my time attacking small tasks and let the big ones slide. For example, my focus at work should have been on writing a quarterly update that I had to present to our upper management, but I was procrastinating and spending my time on less significant tasks.

When I talked to a mentor about my hectic but unproductive days, she was very blunt with me. She said, "You need to choose the things that really matter to you." I realized that I was falling into the same trap of failing to set boundaries that I had back when I was at Coke—it was just manifesting itself differently this time around. I saw once again that setting boundaries and communicating them kindly and clearly was more effective than taking on too much and regretting it later.

I work best when I have a specific plan to follow, so once I was determined to be better at setting boundaries, I needed to impose a structure to force myself to create and maintain them. This meant taking an objective and honest look at where I wanted to focus my time and energy. Once I had that figured out, I could come up with a plan to cut down on the commitments that weren't aligned with my priorities.

I sat down at my desk, and on a big piece of paper I drew two lines—one vertical and one horizontal. In each of the four squares I wrote down an area of my life that was important to me. They were: Me, Friends & Family, Career, and the World. Then, in each square, I wrote my top priorities related to that part of my life, limiting myself to a maximum of three priorities per square. I knew this would force me to say no to things to maintain my boundaries. My goal was to allow these priorities to take up the majority of my time (ideally around 80%) and to allocate the rest of my time to administrative tasks that needed to be taken care of.

But when I took a step back and looked at my squares, it was clear to me right away that my calendar and to-do list were not aligned with the priorities I had identified. I began shifting my schedule and commitments by saying no to and delegating some of the requests that were not aligned.

Over time, this Four Square Model has become an essential

tool in helping me create boundaries and stick with them. Since I started using it, the amount of time I devote to each square has shifted from month to month. Some months are more weighted toward my career; others are filled with family obligations. I do a check-in every two weeks to make sure that my calendar is mapping back to my stated priorities. On a quarterly basis, I also completely revisit my Four Square to determine if I need to change any of my priorities. This is what it looks like right now:

ME	FAMILY
• Cardio	• Caregiver transition
• Meditation	• New experiences
CAREER	WORLD
• Book	• Girl Be Heard fundraiser
• Sale of startup in my portfolio	• School district foundation planning

Of course, these are just my four squares. Yours will be different. Think about the areas of your life that are most important right now. Career (or school, if you're still in college or graduate school) will almost always be one of the four. The others may be the same as mine or they may be filled with: a hobby, side hustle, or passion project that brings you great joy; travel; social or political advocacy; continuing your education; or a particular relationship.

Even with my Four Square Model, it is still a constant struggle to balance my time among all of my responsibilities and passions, especially as a working mom. I am often asked in interviews how I manage to "balance everything," or how I "do it all," and my honest answer is that I don't. Instead, I try to do my best at those priorities that really matter to me. The Four Square Model simply helps me define and constantly re-evaluate what those things are.

I recently sat down with a mentee named Sarah, who is in her mid-twenties and works as a media planner at an ad agency, and helped her create her own Four Square. Sarah's squares were: Me, Friends & Family, Career, and Political Advocacy. We started by talking about her current priorities. She was thinking about dipping her toe into politics by joining the campaign team for her friend's father, who was running for mayor in her hometown. She also had a close friend who'd just broken up with her boyfriend of four years, and Sarah wanted to prioritize spending time with her friend over the next couple of months. In her career, Sarah realized she hadn't spent enough time building her network, so she wanted to make that a priority. She also had a personal health issue that she needed to put front and center in her "me" square.

Next, we looked at Sarah's calendar and to-do list for the last month and realized that she was spending only about a quarter of her time on the things that mattered to her. She needed to reshape her calendar and her to-do list, which meant taking a hard look at what she was going to drop. Sarah was doing a lot of community service for her friend's church youth group, which she felt good about, but it wasn't aligned with her priorities. She decided to reduce her commitment to that in order to focus on the political campaign.

We looked at how she could stop spending so much time attending various youth group meetings and events and instead help in small yet impactful ways. She told her friend, "I have so much on my plate, but I'd love to help you. I have a relationship with a local news editor I can introduce you to so that you can work on getting the group some press coverage." Again, she drew a boundary while being thoughtful and helpful and without leaving anyone hanging.

Meanwhile, at work, one of Sarah's peers was spearheading a project to revamp the corporate cafeteria and had recruited Sarah to join her. This was taking up a lot of time, but it wasn't helping her reach her professional goals because there was no one on that team who could help Sarah from a networking perspective. We talked about how Sarah could extricate herself without leaving the team hanging. She had another friend at work that she knew would benefit from forming a relationship with someone on the team, so Sarah went to her friend and asked if she'd like to take her place. Then she went to the team leader and said, "This is something I'd love to be helpful with, and I'm grateful for the opportunity, but I need to focus on other pressing things right now. The good news is that I've already lined up a great replacement."

Setting Boundaries in Your Career Square

Work-life balance is a battle for everyone, especially women, and while it's a subject that I care deeply about, it's not the focus of this particular book. I recommend Tiffany Dufu's *Drop the Ball* and Anne-Marie Slaughter's *Unfinished Business* for specific advice on this topic. Here, I'll focus on how to create boundaries to protect your time at work so that you can spend the bulk of your time on the top priorities in your career square. Here are some of the techniques that have worked for me:

Get Clear on Your Goals

When I originally created my Four Square and got to the square for Career, I found myself wanting to write down a million things. Limiting myself to only three items helped me clarify my top priorities, which were: acquisitions (identifying companies to acquire in the e-commerce space), leveraging social media to grow our audience, and achieving our revenue goals.

Before you can begin to create boundaries, you need clarity on your priorities based on your company's goals and your own personal career goals. This will help you decide what to say yes to and what to delegate, decline, or put on the back burner. If you're not sure what your priorities at work should be, take a stab at it and run it by your boss. Try saying, "This is what I think I should be focusing on based on the company's goals. Does this look right to you?"

Don't stop there. You need to know what success looks like for everything you take on so that you can prioritize accordingly. If you're assigned to a project and in the kickoff meeting there's no definitive discussion of what success looks like, raise your hand and ask: "What does success look like for this project? What is going to make us feel great when we're done?" That kind of direct question will go a long way toward helping everyone visualize the specific target goal.

Create Filters

Once I knew which three items I needed to focus on (acquisitions, social media, and revenue), I saw that I needed to find a way to cut out extraneous tasks so I could spend the majority of my time on these items. By that point in my career, I had over a hundred people on my team at Time, Inc. To prioritize, I needed to create filters.

For example, I decided to only go out on a sales call if it was either with a strategic partner for the company or if the potential deal would bring in over a certain amount of revenue. When it came to startups that wanted to meet with me, my policy was that I'd take a meeting with the CEO or else I'd delegate it to someone on my team.

I called the list of things that I wasn't going to do because they were filtered out using these criteria my "to-don't list." Looking at this list was absolutely freeing. It became much easier to make decisions and say no to people because I was simply adhering to my predetermined personal policy.

I used this same technique when it came to my philanthropic work. I'm so passionate about philanthropy that it's very easy for me to say yes to everything and spread myself way too thin. When I found myself on the host committee for three different fundraisers and the board of directors for two organizations, I knew it was time to create a filter. Taking a step back, I decided I was most passionate about empowering girls and women, and I decided to focus primarily on philanthropic work in those areas.

Finding this clarity was really beneficial for me. It took the stress and agony out of decision-making about which initiatives to support. Best of all, it gave me an easy and honest way to say a kind no to requests that fell outside of this filter: "This sounds like a wonderful cause, but I've chosen to focus on organizations that empower women and girls, as this is where I've found I can add the most value."

To create your own filters, go back to the goals and priorities you listed on your Four Square. If a meeting or task will help you meet one of your goals in any way, it's an automatic yes. If not, before saying no, carefully consider who is making the request. If it's your boss or someone more senior who may be helpful to you down the road, it's also a yes because it will help you grow your network. If you're in a more junior position, I understand that it may not be possible for you to say no to the tasks that others (e.g., your bosses) are asking you to do. In this case, your filters will be helpful in prioritizing your daily to-do list.

It's a good idea to get your boss's buy-in once you have applied your filters. You've already gotten his or her approval of your goals, so you should be on the same page about which tasks are the most important. During your next meeting, try saying, "I really want to make sure I'm making the best use of my time, and I realized that I was devoting too much time to X, Y, and Z, but they're not adding value to the company. I wanted to let you know that I'm planning on deprioritizing those things unless you think they're adding more value than I realize."

Set Fences Around Your Schedule

Once you know what your specific goals are, it's essential to protect the time you need to devote to meeting them. My solution has been to set strict fences around my schedule to protect the time I spend focusing on creative tasks.

As I transitioned from a traditional corporate job to working for myself, this has become even more important. Many of the young women I mentor who work as consultants or freelancers have also benefitted from setting strict boundaries to make the most of their time. This can be very difficult when juggling multiple clients who each think they should be your top priority.

A young woman I mentor who is a marketing consultant told me that she sets boundaries by focusing on only one client on a given day and not checking email while she works. This method helps her stay in her flow and be more productive. If something urgent comes up, she asks her clients to text her, but only if it's about something that is truly time sensitive. When setting these expectations up front, she makes it clear that this is how she does her best work.

Here's what works for me: whenever possible, from 9 a.m. to 12 p.m., I disconnect from social media, close my email, and put my phone in airplane mode. It's amazing how much more work you get done when you're not constantly being distracted by text messages and social media updates. I also set fences around my weekly schedule by setting as many meetings as possible on the one or two days a week that I'm in the office. And I try to keep one entire day free of meetings and phone calls so I can really dig into the big projects that require my attention.

If you can't implement something like this because you work in an environment where you're expected to respond to emails immediately, that's okay; you still have a couple of options. First, you can set your phone to "do not disturb" and then go into your settings and select whom you want to receive calls or texts from (such as your boss). This way, your phone will only ring if your boss is trying to reach you. If your boss normally contacts you via email, set an out of office message that says, "I'm heads down working on a deadline. If this is urgent, please text me at xxx-xxx-xxxx."

Alternatively, you can respond to an email from your boss by saying: "I'm making so much progress on this project, and I can't wait to share it with you. Can I get back to you on this other topic later today?" This sends a clear yet nice message that you want to be left alone to focus.

Perform an Airplane View

Over the weekend, I look at my calendar for the upcoming week and evaluate whether or not the meetings and calls I have scheduled align with my priorities. If not, I do one of four things to get some of that essential time back: delegate, cancel, reschedule, or shorten the meeting.

Another tactic is to question recurring meetings. So many meetings are scheduled simply because that's how things have always been done. Take a look at the recurring meetings you attend every week and ask yourself if they're really necessary. If you're not the one scheduling the meetings, why not try raising this issue with the person who is? Say, "I'm concerned that I have all these recurring meetings on my calendar. A lot of them are in the morning, and I find that is when I do my best work. Is it possible to move some of these meetings to the afternoon?"

A lot of the women I mentor would never think to raise issues like this, but in general, you should never be afraid to bring up an issue as long as it stems from an authentic desire to make sure you're doing your best work.

Avoid "The Creep"

One thing I hear over and over from the young women I mentor is that they've negotiated flexible hours at work or even taken a pay cut in exchange for part-time hours (such as 80% of their salary to work four days a week instead of five), yet their work hours magically creep up over time, and eventually, they end up working full time without being compensated for it. Then they don't know how to raise this issue without coming across as selfish or lazy.

No doubt this is a tricky situation. I always advise these women to nip it in the bud as early as possible and set expectations so their bosses don't get accustomed to them being available 24/7 and then resent it when they cut back. This is one reason that boundaries are even *more* important than usual when you have a flexible or freelance work arrangement. If you negotiate a flexible schedule, set clear boundaries right away using all of the advice in this chapter, and then make an effort to maintain them as closely as possible. If you see your work hours starting to creep up, address it with your boss quickly: "I'd like to talk about going back to our original agreement of working four days a week."

I understand that it can be hard to bring this up without fearing that it will be held against you, but remember — your boss already agreed to this and hired you with this boundary in mind. You're actually doing her a favor by reminding her to stick to her own boundaries!

Get Rid of the Time Sucks

While you're creating your "to-don't list," make sure to add all the little time sucks that add up and keep your schedule out of alignment with your priorities. If you're not sure what these are, try keeping track of how you're spending your time for a few days. Then look at your time log and ask yourself: *"What can I delegate, delete, or even barter?"*

So many of the young women I mentor barter tasks with their friends and acquaintances. For example, a young woman who was right out of law school asked her friend who was a web designer to create a website for her burgeoning law practice. In exchange, she reviewed her friend's contracts with new clients. I think this is a great way to inexpensively delegate tasks in exchange for something you enjoy or that comes more naturally to you.

In her book *Thrive*, Arianna Huffington talks about learning to cross something off her to-do list simply by deciding not to do it. I love this idea. We all have so many things that we feel we "should" do, but do we really have to do them? If you've been meaning to do something and you haven't gotten around to it, maybe that's because it's actually out of alignment with your priorities. If that's the case, then cross it off your list and consider it done. You've just freed up more time for the things that really matter.

For example, when I was at Time, Inc., I had it on my to-do list to reformat a weekly report that went out to my team, but I never managed to find time to do it. Other tasks kept taking precedence. Finally, I realized that this was because the formatting of the report wasn't really that important. It was an internal document, and it was the content that truly mattered. So I crossed this task off of my list and never looked back.

How to Deliver a "Kind No"

By now, you have some ideas about where to draw your boundaries and how to set them up. Now, it's time to maintain them. When a request for your time comes in that falls outside of your boundaries (in other words, it's been filtered out by the criteria you set), this means just saying no.

This is where a lot of "nice girls" struggle. They wonder how they can say no without damaging the relationship with this person. There have been times—I admit, even recently—when I tried to avoid saying no and ended up making things so much worse. A company founder recently reached out to me through a mutual friend. I took an initial call, and he followed up by asking for an introduction to someone in my network. I made the introduction, and then he followed up by asking for another one.

At this point, I had been helpful to him in a way that felt good to me, but I wasn't willing to devote any more time to his company. But instead of simply telling him this, I'm embarrassed to say that I ignored his email, hoping he'd get the hint, because I didn't want to say no. He emailed me a few days later saying that he appreciated how helpful I'd been thus far and hoped I was comfortable continuing to make introductions. He also asked if I'd be interested in coming on board as a formal advisor.

This forced me to be clear with him. I wrote, "Thank you for the opportunity to be involved in such a great company. I've had to cut back on my advising to focus on my book, so I can't take this on right now, but I wish you the best of luck." Notice that I said, "thank you," instead of, "I'm sorry"! He responded graciously, and I was grateful. This interaction reinforced the fact that a "kind no" is always possible and always better than no answer at all.

There are many ways of delivering a "kind no." You've already read many examples throughout this chapter, and I'm constantly learning new ways to nicely yet clearly assert my boundaries. Pat Hedley, a fellow advisor and investor, recently told me, "Whenever I am asked to do something that I know I cannot accomplish with the utmost quality, I say, 'I can't do this because I won't be able to allocate the time and effort needed to be successful and to do the very best job possible. I would never want to disappoint or fall short of expectations.' Better to say no than to do a bad job. When positioned in this way, people understand and appreciate why I have to say no." I couldn't have said it better.

Here are some additional ways of phrasing a "kind no" so you can make sure that your boundaries and relationships at work remain intact:

- "I would love to help, but right now I'm focusing on . . ."
- "Thank you so much for thinking of me. I'd love to work with you, but my plate is completely full for the next quarter. Please think of me again the next time you have an opportunity."
- "I wish I could help, but I'm not sure I'm the right person for this. You need someone who focuses on . . ."
- "I feel really comfortable doing the X part. I think it would be so much more efficient for someone who's an expert in Y to handle that."
- "I'd love to see you, but I'm heads down building my business. Can we reconnect over the summer?"

Own Your No

You've probably noticed the huge trend in the media these days, telling women to step up, go for it, lean in, and say yes. And while that's certainly an improvement over the messages that were sent to previous generations of women, it's not always realistic. In fact, this type of extra intense encouragement sometimes makes women feel that we must say yes to every opportunity or else we'll be missing out, or worse, become bad feminists. FOMO, anyone? But the truth is that sometimes the best decision *is* no, even if it means turning down a big opportunity.

As I was writing this book, three companies were pursuing me about taking on a big operating role. I'll be honest — my ego loved to think about how it would look to others if I accepted one of these jobs. But then I took my own advice and took a moment to visualize what every day would look like if I did. I'd be commuting over an hour each way into New York City every day. On days when I didn't have a work event at night, I'd see my kids for thirty minutes. On days when I did have an event, I wouldn't see them at all. That is not what I want — at least not right now. Though it was difficult to make, I have learned to own this decision, knowing that circumstances may change and something different may be right for me at some point in the future.

I do not feel like I'm choosing between my family and my career, nor am I advocating that any woman should feel like she has to choose. It's not either/or. But I also have no interest in echoing the same old mantra that women can "have it all." Instead of trying to have it all (whatever that even means), we need to reshape what it means for us to be invested in our careers. Right now, for me it doesn't have to mean working at a big company. (I also know how fortunate I am to be able to make that decision. It took me over two decades of putting in long hours to reach the point where I can shape my career to suit my needs.)

In *Lean In*, Sheryl Sandberg encourages women to have a big career. And I don't disagree. But first we have to redefine what having a big career means. Sometimes, when you're defining that for yourself, saying no is the right decision.

The Sweet Spot in Between Yes and No

Requests for your time, energy, or expertise often seem like yes or no propositions, but I've found that there is actually plenty of space to be helpful in between yes and no. It's all about saying, "I can't do that now, but here's what I *can* do . . ." Often, this is the sweet spot for adding value without doing heavy lifting. Over time, I have gotten more and more comfortable taking this approach and have found that it's the perfect combination of being giving while protecting my own time and boundaries.

I use this technique most often at work, but it has come in handy in many different situations, most recently with the PTA at my sons' school. This year, they asked me to co-chair the big annual fundraising gala. But I knew that running the auction, as I had the year before, would be a much better fit for me, so I told them, "I think the best role for me to play is to run the auction again. It's a ton of work, but I have all the processes down, and it's easy to get stuff donated given the work I do and the relationships I have. I'm confident that we can put together a great auction committee based on the ladies who did it last year, and I have a few new moms that I've already recruited to help. I think it would be great to have one or two co-chairs that are running the entire event, and I will be their point person on the auction."

It made me smile when the PTA vice president responded by saying, "I totally understand. In fact, I could learn a thing to two from you about acknowledging when it's time to know you're stretched and not overcommit! So thrilled to have you on to chair the auction."

To give you a better idea of how to do this, here are some of my go-to responses when my answer isn't quite a yes or a no. They can be adapted to any situation. The point is that I try to be respectful and offer an alternative way to help that is less time intensive than the initial ask.

- As a mentor (to a young woman asking to go out for coffee and "pick my brain"): "I would love to have you join me for an upcoming mentor circle. We get ten to fifteen women together, and magic usually happens." Or try saying, "I'd love to. I'm heads down working on an important project at work. Can we reconnect in a few months?" (Then leave it to them to reach back out to you.)
- As a networker (to someone asking me to introduce them to a person in my network): "I'd love to introduce you. Can you write an email about yourself and why you're interested in speaking that I can forward to her?"
- As a job candidate (to a hiring manager or recruiter who is offering you a job that you don't want to take): "This job isn't the

right fit for me right now, but I have two people in mind who would be great candidates. I'd be happy to connect you with them."

- As an advisor (to a founder who wants to meet with me): "I've pressed pause on formal advising for the next six months while I'm working on a book, but I'm happy to spend twenty minutes on the phone if you're looking for specific advice." This offer to spend a limited amount of time on the phone is a great way to be giving to anyone who's looking to get on your calendar without spending a lot of time meeting with someone in person — plus the time it would take for you to get there and back.
- As a friend (to a friend who's hosting an event that she wants me to attend): "Unfortunately, I can't make it, but I'd love to help you promote the event on social media."

Key Takeaways

- Before drawing boundaries, it's important to first identify your priorities so you can make sure to devote your time to activities that are in alignment with them.
- To do this, I created a Four Square Model — and every few months, I revisit my priorities and make sure my time is being allocated appropriately.
- When obligations come up that fall outside of your priorities, try to respond with a clear but kind no. Or, if possible, delegate the task so you have time to focus on other priorities.
- There is a sweet spot in between yes and no. When something is asked of you, think about whether or not there is a better, more efficient way for you to add value.

9

Multiply Your Superpower

As you can probably tell from many of the stories in this book, mentorship is a big part of my life. In part, it is so important to me because early on in my career I didn't have any professional mentors. My parents were incredibly loving and supportive in every way, but they were immigrants with no contacts in or knowledge about the business world. They couldn't advise me or put me in touch with professional mentors.

Then, in college, I met peers whose parents were investment bankers or worked for big companies. They seemed to have a much easier time getting internships and even jobs as soon as they graduated. It was as though they had a built-in mechanism to jumpstart their careers. Meanwhile, I found that I had to learn how to succeed on my own. Looking back, I understand how much easier it would have been if I'd had someone in my corner who was already connected to the business world.

The first person who took an interest in my career path and took on a mentor role in my life was my boss, Lou, at Ernst & Young. He's the one who first told me that I needed to voice my opinions in meetings instead of just saying, "That's interesting!" In that company, my colleagues and I moved from team to team, serving different clients based on their needs. I was assigned to work for a client on Lou's team, and it went so well that he booked me to work with him again for another client.

Lou was highly regarded in the company, so he received a lot of the plum assignments. Because he had so much faith in me, I was assigned to some of the company's best clients. Thanks to Lou, I saw firsthand how impactful it was to have someone like him looking out for me.

Finally finding a mentor was like having a teacher who really "got" me. He saw my strengths and helped me play to them while also filling in the gaps in my knowledge and experience. Overall, this mentoring relationship gave me a tremendous amount of confidence and know-how early on in my career.

That's the essence of what a mentor can do for you. He or she is that individual whose guidance and counsel you not only learn from, but also fully trust. Whenever you have tricky or difficult decisions to make, it's a wonderful feeling to know that you can reach out to your mentor as a safety net and source of support.

In short, finding and developing a relationship with a mentor —or numerous mentors—is critical to your rise in the business world. Yet, many of the young women I speak to tell me that finding a mentor can be extremely difficult, especially if they are hesitant or insecure about asking for help or requesting someone's time. I'm often surprised by how many women I speak to who don't have (and have never had) a mentor.

Sure enough, LinkedIn conducted a survey in 2011 that found only one in five women had ever had a professional mentor. This is a big problem when you consider the research showing that, all else being equal, having a mentor can be the "X factor" that helps launch your career forward.

Here's what some of the women I surveyed said about the challenge to find a mentor at work:

- "I've always wanted to find a mentor, but I work in a niche industry with very few women and have never figured out how to find the right person."
- "Sometimes, I meet women in my industry who offer to meet with me, but I can't tell if they really mean it or if they're just being nice, so sometimes I don't follow up. Then I end up wondering if I've missed out on a big opportunity."
- "I have a mentor at my company, but sometimes it seems like when she gives me advice she is thinking more about what's good for the company than what's good for me. Do I need to find someone outside the company who can be more objective?"

Identifying the Right Mentor

The process of connecting to a mentor is very similar to the process of networking that you read about in Chapter 7. But before you start networking to find a mentor, it's important to identify the *right* mentor—one (or more) who can expertly help guide you toward success. Many of the young women I speak to assume that their bosses will mentor them, but that's not always the case. Furthermore, your boss is not necessarily the best mentor for you (though he or she very well may be).

Think about the people in your life who have successfully blended kindness with strength. Who do you admire and want to be like? When you think back to your most impactful teachers and coaches, they're rarely the ones who let you get away with murder *or* the ones who were nasty and discouraging. They're the ones who were kind yet firm and helped you thrive. This is the best type of mentor.

That's right—not all mentors are created equal. To get the most out of this relationship, it's important to be intentional about whom you will approach to become your mentor. To make this process simple, I've broken it down into three steps:

Step 1: Find Your Type

Start by asking yourself what type of mentor you're looking for. From my experience, a mentee is usually looking for at least one of these three characteristics in a mentor:

1. *Power to help you advance in your career.* If this is what you need, start by looking at the people in senior positions in your company. When I was at Time, Inc., young women often reached out to me because they knew I was in a powerful position to help them move up within the company.

2. *An influential network.* If your goal is to network your way to new opportunities, perhaps you need a mentor who is extremely well connected and also willing to act as a gateway to other people.

3. *Expertise.* This can be a specific skill set (such as leadership or managerial skills if you're transitioning into a manager role), knowledge about the inner workings of a particular company or industry, or experience dealing with a certain type of situation. For example, many young women reach out to me to find out how I made the transition from media to investing. My experience making this transition has given me expertise that they can learn from if they are contemplating something similar.

Reading this, you may realize that you need a mentor with one, two, or even all three of these attributes. You may need three separate mentors to get all three, or you might luck out and find one mentor with all of them. In general, it's wonderful to have more than one mentor to give you multiple perspectives, but these relationships do take time and energy. Be intentional and try to find a small handful of mentors who can make the biggest possible impact.

Step 2: Go In or Out

Once you've identified the type of mentor you're looking for, think about whether that person should be within your current company or on the outside. If you love working at the company and your goal is to keep advancing internally, then it's best to look for someone powerful within the company. If, however, you're looking to transition to another company or even a different industry, your ideal mentor will be someone on the outside.

If you're unsure of what your exact goals are, but you do know that you're eager to move on from your current situation, it may be helpful to network and find mentors who exist completely outside of your universe. A fresh perspective can get you thinking about the infinite number of possibilities that are out there. For example, connecting with Soraya Darabi (who you read about in Chapter 7) gave me insight about and access to the tech world, which was critical to me eventually making that transition.

We often get stuck thinking that our mentor has to be someone in our particular silo, but that can be unnecessarily limiting. The ideal mentor may be right in front of you without you realizing it. Think about all of the people you are already connected to. If you're just starting out in your career, it can be an old professor, an acquaintance, or even someone you used to babysit for. Do any of those people have power, access, or expertise that can help you? If not, perhaps they are connected to someone else who does. This all ties back to networking. You never know how someone may be helpful down the road, so it's always a good idea to broaden your horizons (and your network) as much as possible.

Step 3: Assess Their Interest in Mentoring

Not everyone is a good mentor, and for that matter, not everyone *wants* to be a good mentor. A good mentor is someone who enjoys it and feels that it's a natural part of his or her job. Once you've identified the type of mentor you're looking for and whether he or she is inside or outside of your company, it's important to assess a potential mentor's penchant for mentorship.

If you think that your boss would be an ideal mentor, pay attention to whether or not he or she asks a lot of insightful questions and provides support. If so, your search may be over, but if he or she focuses more on getting the work done and doesn't volunteer advice or guidance, it may be best to look elsewhere.

In this case, start paying attention to how your peers and friends speak about their own bosses and mentors. Perhaps you have a friend who raves about how helpful her boss is. Or maybe a peer works for someone you think would make a good mentor, but your friend's feedback is that while she's very powerful and connected, mentoring really isn't her thing.

Another good way to go about this is to ask your boss about someone he or she knows: "I'm looking to learn more about [Insert Topic] and I thought [Name] could provide some great insights and guidance. What do you think?" If your boss doesn't think that the person you mentioned would make a good mentor, it's very likely that he or she can suggest someone else who would!

Connect to a Mentor

Now that you know the exact type of mentor you're looking for and where you may find him or her, how will you make the connection and stand out among all the other people who may be vying for this person's attention? Here are some of the techniques I've found to be most effective:

Get a Warm Introduction

I discussed this briefly in Chapter 7, but it bears repeating—being personally introduced to a potential mentor by a mutual friend or acquaintance will carry a lot of weight and make you stand out far more than sending a cold email. Casually drop this into conversations with colleagues and friends: "One thing I'm focusing on right now is finding a mentor who can help me with . . ." or, "I think [Name] would be an ideal mentor as I transition into a managerial role. Do you think she'd be willing to meet with me?" Hopefully one of the people you mention this to will be willing to make a warm introduction to the right person.

Another effective way to find mutual contacts is to go onto LinkedIn and other social media sites and see whom your connections are connected to. Then reach out and offer to write an email that he or she can forward to your potential mentor. This makes it easier for them, and therefore more likely that he or she will actually do it.

In this introductory email, make sure it's clear that the meeting will be mutually beneficial rather than parasitic. Instead of a basic, "I'd love to meet so I can pick your brain and learn more about your experience," here's what one woman wrote to me recently: "I've been following your career and am a big fan. I'm currently in transition and am so impressed with your move from media to investing. I would love to learn more about your experience, and in return, I have some ideas on how Company X in your portfolio can grow its audience based on my experience in digital marketing."

See how much more powerful and compelling that is? She had done her research about my career trajectory and offered to share her expertise in a specific and helpful way in exchange for my time.

Find a Personal Point of Connection

If you can't find someone to make a warm introduction for you, don't worry. There are other ways to successfully connect with a potential mentor. I recently received a "cold" email that started with, "I see that we both used to live in Mount Kisco. It's so beautiful up there . . ." The idea that we had something in common made me want to keep reading. This requires doing a little research beforehand, but it's bound to pay off.

Create a Moment

A very savvy young woman recently put together a panel discussion about women in technology at her company and then reached out to me asking if I'd like to attend. I did, and when I arrived, she introduced herself and made a point of chatting with me as I got settled and found my seat. I was motivated to connect with her because we'd already emailed back and forth about the event. Sure enough, she emailed me a few days later thanking me for attending the event and asking to meet with me. It seemed that she had created the entire event to give herself an opportunity to network with influential panelists and audience members. Plus, of course, the panel was a win for her company. I was so impressed with this strategy that I agreed to meet her for coffee!

If that seems like too large-scale and complex of a process just to get a coffee date, think about other existing "moments" or events that you can use to connect with a potential mentor. I recently got an email from yet another young woman asking to meet with me who used a unique and really effective tactic. Instead of requesting a meeting, she asked, "Will you be at any conferences, networking events, or speaking engagements coming up where we can meet?" This made it so easy for me to meet with her because I didn't have to find time on my calendar. I simply told her about a few events I was already planning on attending, and she showed up. This made a great impression on me, which means I'll probably be more likely to say yes to a meeting the next time she asks.

Get Noticed

When I think about the early days of my career, which took place before social media and online networking existed, I see that I was able to find many valuable mentors because I simply did good work that stood out to them. They wanted to mentor me because they saw my potential. Of course, the other tips in this section are important, and you need to pick your head up from your desk to network and put yourself out there, but nothing can fully replace the value of over-delivering in a way that will really make you stand out. Review Chapter 2 for advice on how to step up and create opportunities that will help you get noticed.

Form a Personal Board of Directors

Adaora Udoji, who, as you read earlier, bravely spoke up to an interviewer who said she didn't look like a tax lawyer, refers to her group of mentors and mentees as her "personal board of directors." She told me the biggest mistake a young woman can make is thinking that she can figure everything out by herself. You need a diverse group of people you've developed relationships with to round out your experience and expertise.

Adaora suggests looking at the people who are already in your life who you respect instead of going out and seeking a "board member." Who have you spent time with over the last five years and learned from? Who responds to your emails and seems eager to offer their support? Her board has been invaluable to Adaora, and I love this unique approach to mentorship.

Asking to Pick Someone's Brain
Is the Kiss of Death

When you are looking to engage a mentor, it's important to approach the person (either in person or virtually) in a way that cannot be construed as exploitative or entitled. Remember, this person does not owe you anything. Even if she is authentically kind and giving, she's probably also extremely busy and keenly aware of how valuable her time and expertise is.

Instead of thinking about what you can gain from this person, think about how to build a relationship with him or her. This means that, as Sheryl Sandberg said in *Lean In*, never approach a stranger and ask him or her to be your mentor. It's crucial to allow the relationship to develop organically. As a "nice girl," you have an advantage here because building relationships probably comes naturally to you. Now is the time to leverage that skill to maximize your success.

Even more important, though, than not outright asking someone to be your mentor, is never, ever asking someone to "pick their brain." My friend Tereza Nemessanyi recently wrote about this on Facebook in a post that really hit home for me while making me laugh. She said:

"Professional Networking PSA: DO NOT use the term 'pick your brain.' Just don't. There is a lot of agreement on this among heavy networkers. Here's the issue:

'Pick your brain' is non-reciprocal and exploitative. People who hear this a lot tend to cringe. These people are super time constrained and need to see something in it for them. The offer of coffee does not make it more attractive. Somehow, this wording has amped up in the last month or so, after having receded for a few years. It's a problem. Instead: make it reciprocal ('feedback'/'brainstorm'), make it QUICK and easy (a 20-min phone call, not in-person coffee), and at the close, ask how you can be helpful in return. Please share this out, friends. We need to break the chain."

Be Open to Unlikely Mentors

While it's important to be intentional about finding a mentor, sometimes mentors show up where you least expect them. When you're open to this, you can receive meaningful advice and support from people you never would have thought to seek out for that purpose.

Susan Canavari, the chief brand officer at JPMorgan Chase, shared a wonderful story with me about finding a mentor in an unexpected place. In 2002, she was working at Digitas and was asked to move to California to run their San Francisco office. Her job was to assess how they could grow the business and motivate the current team after experiencing a rough period with a lot of turnover in the previous five years.

Susan showed up on her first day and was greeted by forty-nine skeptical people plus one positive one—Betreda Gaines, the head of HR for the San Francisco office. Betreda had been through the upheaval of the last several leaders and had seen it all. Though Susan was technically her superior, Betreda had valuable insights into their unique office culture. And so, the head of HR became a mentor to the head of the entire office. She confided in Susan about why people were so skeptical about her coming to San Francisco and coached her on what she could do and say to gain the staff's trust in her plan to make the office a success.

In addition to offering advice that was specific to that office's culture, Betreda did everything she could to make sure Susan led the team in the most effective way. She drafted communications and made sure Susan expressed a consistent message of hope and positivity. Susan told me that she now thinks about that advice every day and always tries to be as loyal and generous as Betreda herself. When Betreda passed away in March of 2017, she left behind a beautiful legacy of kindness and mentorship.

What Is — And Isn't — A Mentor?

While mentorship can take on many forms and come from unexpected places, there are some limitations to what a mentor can and should do. I find that many young women come to me asking me to be their mentor without a clear understanding of precisely what the relationship should entail. Here are some basic guidelines for healthy and productive mentorships:

A MENTOR IS A CASUAL RELATIONSHIP THAT DEVELOPS ORGANICALLY, NOT A FORMAL ARRANGEMENT.

A lot of "nice girls" ask me how often they should reach out to a mentor. They want to keep the relationship alive without overstepping and feeling like a bother. I always emphasize to them that this is not a formal relationship. For instance, there is a big difference in my relationships with the founders I formally advise and the young women I mentor.

As an advisor, I have a formal agreement to meet and speak with them at a predetermined regularity. With my mentees, it's not like that at all. They often reach out over email or text when they need advice or support, and I try to make time to grab coffee or lunch with them at least once every few months.

In addition, I really appreciate it when my mentees continue to engage with me even when they don't need anything. For example, a young woman I mentor recently emailed me an article that she thought I would find interesting, and another sent me a link to an event that she wanted to make sure I knew about. These gestures show me that I'm on their minds and keep our relationship alive in between our deeper discussions.

A MENTOR IS A SOURCE OF GUIDANCE, NOT A DECISION-MAKER FOR YOU.

You should never expect a mentor to tell you what to do. He or she is there to provide wisdom, ideas, advice, information, and a fresh perspective. But at the end of the day, you are responsible for your own decisions.

Caroline Ghosn, the founder and CEO of Levo, said it best: "If your life is a book, then as a mentee, engaging mentors is about finding really thoughtful subjects to interview and editors to remind you of why you're writing a book. But you are the author."

A MENTOR IS OBJECTIVE, NOT SOMEONE WHO'S PERSONALLY INVESTED IN YOUR DECISIONS.

It can be tempting to go to your direct boss or someone else who's very close to you for advice, but that advice often comes filtered through the other person's priorities and opinions—and sometimes even their own insecurities or grudges. The best mentors are able to be objective and point out hidden intricacies, politics, or other aspects of a situation that you may not be aware of. As Caroline Ghosn says, "A mentor is someone who is willing to give you advice that isn't in their own best interest. It takes a real mentor to put you first."

When a mentor is truly objective, it's far easier for him or her to notice the unique skills you bring to the table and opportunities for you to put those skills to work. For example, Mari Kuraishi shared a story with me about an early mentor who saw the potential for her to make the most of her unique skills. Mari was in her first real job, which she had gotten strictly on the basis of her knowledge of Russia. She had zero knowledge about the work of the World Bank, her new employer. But she had a great relationship with her boss, Yukon, a laconic Chinese-American economist who was smart and pragmatic.

At twenty-five, Mari was usually the only woman in every meeting she attended and almost always the youngest. One day, Yukon pulled her aside and asked, "Mari, why don't you ever say anything in the meetings you're in?" She told him that she figured other people's opinions were more valuable than hers and that someone else usually got around to expressing her point of view. To Mari's surprise, Yukon told her that she had knowledge about how things worked in Russia that none of the other people in the room did and that even if someone else eventually expressed what she had to say, she had to be heard saying it.

Mari was shocked. It had never occurred to her that her knowledge of how Russian institutions might constrain the behavior of their clients mattered to her colleagues in the room. Nor had it dawned on her that she needed to be known to them as the person who had that knowledge. To this day, Mari credits that boss for taking enough interest in the most junior professional on his team to tell her to speak up — and later to sponsor her for a mid-career executive MBA, one of the biggest perks that the World Bank had to offer — and in the process helping her become the social entrepreneur she is today. It was his objectivity that helped her see where she could add value and understand how it would help her career to do so.

A MENTOR IS SOMEONE WHO ALSO GAINS FROM THE RELATIONSHIP, NOT SOMEONE WHO ONLY GIVES.
True mentorship is not a one-way street. It's a dynamic relationship in which advice, information, and support flows both ways. Many people think of mentorship in terms of an older, more experienced professional giving advice to someone who's more junior than him or her. But I've learned that I have just as much to learn and gain from my mentees as I have to teach them.

A few years ago, a company in my portfolio was in a tight spot; they had a lot of revenue in the pipeline but were experiencing a momentary shortfall of cash. They clearly weren't going to make it through the next few months without a bridge of financing.

The company was five years old and had already taken in a lot of money. As an investor, I'm constantly on the lookout for companies that could potentially invest in or acquire the startups in my portfolio. As it happened, I had a relationship with a big company that I saw as a potential acquirer of this startup, and I took on the role of negotiating the acquisition.

At this point, I had been through a lot of ups and downs with this startup, and the founder, whom I had mentored for years, could sense my fatigue. She told me, "Fran, when you talk to this company, you need to come from a position of strength."

She was absolutely right, and it was so important for me to hear this from her. Though I was her mentor, in that moment she was mentoring me—and doing so quite effectively. Her advice really helped me have a productive conversation with the company. To me, this is an ideal mentoring relationship—one in which the advice and wisdom flows both ways.

I also often act as a "virtual mentor" on Levo and hold "office hours" when young women can ask me questions through the platform. You might be surprised by how powerful a tiny connection like that can turn out to be. When a woman named Britt Hysen introduced herself to me at a conference, she said, "I'm sure you don't remember, but years ago, I asked you a question about digital media on Levo."

This was a great icebreaker, and surprisingly enough, I *did* remember that question! Britt definitely made an impression on me, and the relationship that stemmed from that interaction has benefitted both of us. We stayed in touch after that initial introduction, and not long afterward, Britt launched *Millennial Magazine* and featured me on the cover as part of their mentor series!

My friend Adaora told me that once she became a mentor, she was surprised by how valuable it was for her. When Adaora was starting out, several more experienced women offered to meet with her and share their wisdom, but she often failed to follow through on these requests because she was worried about overstepping and didn't want to bother them. She was being a people pleaser! Now that she is in a position to mentor younger women, she sees how much she gets out of the experience. Besides energy and inspiration, she gains valuable perspective about what's currently being taught in colleges and universities now, as well as insight into the new sharing economy mentality.

Now, Adaora understands why the women ahead of her wanted to engage with her when she was younger and regrets not taking them up on it. Hating the idea that anyone else will miss out, her advice to you is to take people at their word. "Believe it when people offer," she says. "If it turns out they really don't have the capacity, so be it, but if they offer, grab it with both hands and see what happens; sometimes it will be magic!"

The Mentoring Mindset

Mentoring doesn't always have to happen in a formal setting, and you can become a mentor no matter what stage of your career you're in. In fact, I've given (and received) some of the best advice in casual interactions with a peer. Mark Golin was my peer at Moviefone, AOL, and Time, Inc. He was the creative force, and I ran the business side. We had a relationship that, to me, epitomizes peer mentorship. We respected each other's opinions but never stepped on each other's toes because we brought different skills to the table. We were constantly learning from each other.

My relationship with Mark taught me that mentoring can be a natural way of being, and I've brought that mindset to the teams I've run. To me, the highest compliment is to be thought of as someone who builds effective teams, so I always make it a priority to empower my teams by giving them exposure and sharing the knowledge I've picked up over the course of my career. This isn't just nice; it's also strategic. My team is a reflection of me, and a strong and confident leader knows that she can share her wisdom with those around her and still have value.

Melissa Mattiace, who works in Media Partnerships at Facebook, told me that she likes to think of mentoring as daily interactions that are rooted in kindness, being present, and human connection. She tries to make them a part of her life each day. This crystallized for Melissa recently over lunch with a former colleague named Cathy. Their careers and lives had taken them on different paths, and a few years had passed since they'd last connected.

During their lunch, Cathy shared that she was at a crossroads in her career and was unsure about pursuing a new opportunity that had come up. They discussed the pros and cons of taking her career in this new direction and then mapped them back to Cathy's personal priorities. Then, Melissa suggested that Cathy start out by consulting for the new company so she could road-test the role, rather than commit to it immediately.

A few days later, Melissa received a text that read, "I want to thank you for encouraging me to pursue that opportunity. I've agreed to a two-month project. Our lunch and conversation came at the perfect time; I've always trusted your advice and appreciate you taking the time to talk through things with me."

While they'd always had a great rapport, Melissa had never considered herself a mentor to Cathy. But now she saw that, when strung together, her little acts of kindness had made a bigger impact than she realized.

Can you incorporate moments like this into your daily life? Remember, mentorship is a spectrum. While some mentors are indeed the traditional champions at your place of employment who pave the way for you to make the next step in your career, the truth is, mentors can come in all shapes and sizes. A mentor might be someone who provided you with just the right piece of advice you needed at the moment you needed it. She may be a helpful friend or someone you respect and admire with whom you're engaged in a long-term, mutually supportive relationship. Every type of mentor has different benefits.

It's also important to note that Melissa's former colleague, Cathy, followed up by sharing the impact that Melissa had on her decision-making. This is key to continuing to engage with a mentor and nurturing that relationship over time. If you've made a decision, stood up to a bully, or taken an opportunity thanks in part to advice or support you've received from a mentor, remember to let them know how grateful you are for their wisdom. As a mentor, I love hearing that I've made an impact. Not only does this make me feel good and motivate me to keep going, but it also serves as valuable feedback so that I know where to focus my advice going forward.

Scale Your Mentorship

No matter how much I would like to, I don't have time to meet individually with each person who reaches out to me for mentorship. Plus, I've found that one-on-one interactions aren't always the best way to impart as much knowledge as possible. So, I've looked for creative ways to scale my mentorship so that I can have the greatest possible impact on as many people as I can. These techniques can work at any stage of your career to make valuable connections and dip your toe into the wonderful world of mentorship.

As I mentioned earlier, I regularly host a Mentor Circle, which is a group of about ten to fifteen women. We meet either in a coffee shop or restaurant or the co-working space I use. It's a very informal gathering. We meet for about an hour and get to know each other. I answer questions that come up, but I've seen that it's actually far more beneficial for the women to learn from each other and build peer-to-peer connections.

After noticing this, I've intentionally begun devoting more time during these gatherings for them to interact with each other. Instead of fielding questions, I ask the women to go around in a circle and share something they're working on or struggling with, and I give the other women a chance to respond with thoughts on each struggle before adding my own two cents.

I try to encourage the same dynamic in all sorts of group settings. Caroline Ghosn regularly hosts dinners for diverse groups of people who all get the chance to become mentors for one another. In her book *The Big Life*, my friend Ann Shoket, the former editor-in-chief of *Seventeen*, describes how she hosts "Badass Babes dinner parties" where she gathers millennial women and asks them, "If I could solve any problem for you, what would it be?" The more you follow the networking advice in Chapter 7 and put yourself out there, you'll be amazed by how many of these events you hear about.

But you don't need someone else to host a mentor circle. Why not reach out to some peers who seem interesting and engaged and arrange a networking/peer mentoring event at a local coffee shop, in a conference room at your company's office, or a co-working space? You can loosely structure the event by going around and introducing yourselves and then giving each person a few minutes to share a recent career struggle, goal, or concern. Anyone with advice can weigh in. Another way to structure the event is to have everyone go around and state an offer (something they are willing to help others in the group with) and an ask (something they need from others in the group).

If it's not practical or possible for you to host an event like this, try hosting a Skype conference with a group of like-minded women or using other online platforms such as the "ask me anything" feature on Mogul or even Google Hangouts or Facebook Live.

• • •

My wish is that you'll take everything you learn from your mentors and all the skills you've learned throughout this book and use them to impart wisdom, advice, and support, and spread the power of kindness in service of all the women who will come next. Just by being a strong and kind, ambitious and likeable, empathetic and decisive, confident and flexible woman, you can help turn around the double standards we all face and permanently change the way women at work are perceived. And when the women coming up behind you follow in your footsteps, they'll multiply your kindness exponentially.

Acknowledgments

I can't even begin to express my gratitude to my family, friends, colleagues, mentors, and so many more who have walked this path with me. Your generosity with your wisdom, insights, time, energy, resources, and so much more will always be remembered. I send out great love and heartfelt appreciation to all of you.

Thank you to the more than four hundred women in my network who provided feedback on everything from the title to the topics and stories covered in the book. You know who you are . . . and I'm forever grateful for the time you spent with me on the phone, over email, in groups, and in person.

My deep thanks to my peers and fellow authors who guided me along the way and helped me understand the unexpected ins and outs of writing a book. Your advice and friendship guided me enormously, and I'm so happy I didn't need to reinvent the wheel. I want to especially thank Tiffany Dufu for telling me that "nice is your capital" and giving me the confidence to proceed with the book at a time when I needed it.

In addition, I was fortunate to have a posse of rock star women to interview for the book, all of whom spent precious time sharing stories about pivotal moments in their lives. It's these women who brought the book into real focus with their honesty, vulnerability, and authenticity. My thanks to: Adaora Udoji, Anna Maria Chavez, Caroline Ghosn, Chrissy Carter, Dawn Casale, Emily Dalton, Janet Comenos, Jennifer Fleiss, Josephine D'Ippolito, Kat Cole, Mari Kuraishi, Melissa Mattiace, Mimi Feliciano, Mindy Grossman, Pat Hedley, Soraya Darabi, Stephanie Kaplan Lewis, and Susan Canavari.

So many people provided incredibly valuable insights that enhanced the content in the book. My deep appreciation to all of you: Allison McGuire, Anjali Kumar, Blake Lively, Dayle Haddon, Denise Restauri, Elizabeth Kim, Ellen Miller, Emily Listfield, Grace Prudente, Grace Fedele, Jacqueline Hernandez, Jane Hanson, Jessie Goldberg, Susan McPherson, Vanessa Schenck, and Whitney Frick.

My personal mentors have meant more to me than they will ever know. They have guided me along the way, talked me off numerous ledges, and generously shared their wisdom and insights. My humble thanks to Adam Slutsky, Ann Moore, David Geithner, Lamar Chesney, Mark Golin, Martha Nelson, and Paul Caine.

I'm lucky to have the best marketing team in Amanda Schumacher and Kathleen Harris. Your creativity, energy, and overall brilliance helped me get the message out to the world in an authentic and impactful way. Thank you for believing in the mission and being the ultimate ambassadors. And thank you to Alexis Cambareri and Jennifer Mullowney for helping me put my best face forward (literally) and to Annie Werner, Briana Link, Chris Winfield, Farnoosh Torabi, Melissa Goidel, and Selena Soo for your incredibly valuable guidance on how to best launch the book.

A big thank you to Michelle Rawicz, for keeping me on track and organized and for handling a million miscellaneous things (while making it all look so easy!).

A few of my favorite people were there every step of the way offering me courage, inspiration, and guidance in a multitude of ways. Liz White read an early version of the book and provided so many thoughtful ideas. Jennie Baird is a brilliant and poignant writer herself and crafted the original proposal when it was a completely different book. She continued to provide indispensable support along the way, including helping me to find my writing collaborator, Jodi Lipper. MJ Ryan is my magnificent coach and mentor and played a crucial role in helping me to initially structure the book. My heartfelt appreciation goes out to each of you.

To one of my dearest friends in this world, Patricia Karpas. Patricia has been my closest and most trusted advisor on this since 2009! This book would not have happened if it weren't for her relentless (and I mean that in a good way) encouragement. She has added value every step of the way and has helped me get "unstuck" on many occasions. Patricia, I am so filled with love and admiration for you.

This book could not have come to life in the way that it has without my amazing agent, the incandescent Yfat Reiss Gendell. She has been my pillar from the day we met, and she was the one who convinced me that this was the book I was meant to write. It has been a privilege and honor to work with Yfat and the whole Foundry team, especially Jessica Felleman.

Thanks to the incredibly talented and supportive team at Houghton Mifflin Harcourt, including Ellen Archer, Bruce Nichols, Adriana Rizzo, Maire Gorman, Debbie Engel, Lori Glazer, Hannah Harlow, Martha Kennedy, Christopher Moisan, Beth Burleigh Fuller, Katja Jylkka, Stephanie Buschardt, Rachel Newborn, and Katie Coaster.

I owe a special debt of gratitude to my editor Rick Wolff and editorial associate Rosemary McGuinness. They are beyond brilliant, creative, and fiercely intuitive. They believed deeply in what we were creating together, were my biggest champions, and pushed me (in a nice way, of course) to find just the right way to tell this story.

It has been my personal joy to work with Jodi Lipper, my writing collaborator. Jodi—"thank you" does not seem to do justice to the contributions you made to this book. Your ability to translate my thoughts and experiences into an engaging narrative is everything. Thank you for your deep commitment to and passion for the book, your unbelievable capacity for finding just the right language to tell a story, your patience, kindness, and, now, friendship.

My day begins and ends with the two precious boys who are my sons, Anthony and Will. They make me smile every single day and give my life a deeper meaning than I ever could have imagined. I love you both to pieces.

My dear husband Frank reminds me every day what it means to be in true partnership. He is a loving father and husband, and I'm grateful beyond words that we share our lives together. His support for this book has meant everything to me. Thank you, "Fran with a K." I love you.

To the man, my father Antonio, who brought our family to this country when I was two; who had the courage and quiet strength to build a business before he spoke a word of English; who leads with kindness; and who, with my mother Carmela, created a beautiful family including the best siblings a girl could ask for, Josephine, Rocco, and Nat . . . there are no words.

In life, there are few people who embody the true spirit of love. My mother is one of them. You were my first teacher. Thank you for teaching me how to lead with grace and that being nice is a true gift that one can give the world.

Notes

1. NICE IS YOUR SUPERPOWER

page

8   *Research shows that a positive:* Jonha Revesencio, "Why Happy Employees are 12% More Productive," *Fast Company,* July 22, 2015. https://www.fastcompany.com/3048751/happy-employees-are-12-more-productive-at-work.

    than their unhappy peers: Ibid.

    A recent study from the Harvard Business Review: Rob Cross, Reb Rebele, and Adam Grant, "Collaborative Overload," *Harvard Business Review,* January–February 2016. https://hbr.org/2016/01/collaborative-overload.

13   *Research shows that our instincts:* Amy J.C. Cuddy, Peter Glick, and Anna Beninger, "The dynamics of warmth and competence judgments, and their outcomes in organizations," *Research in Organizational Behavior,* Vol. 31, (2011): 73–98. http://www.hbs.edu/faculty/Pages/item.aspx?num =41451.

    answer these two questions: Ibid.

2. BE AMBITIOUS *AND* LIKEABLE

19   *In one study from the Columbia Business School:* Frank Flynn, remarks to attendees at the Women in Management (WIM) Banquet, January 1, 2007. Published in Joanne Martin, "Gender-Related Material in the New Core Curriculum," Stanford Graduate School of Business (website). https://www.gsb.stanford.edu/stanford-gsb-experience/news-history/gender-related-material-new-core-curriculum.

28   *Studies show that elementary school teachers:* For example, Diane Reay,

"'Spice Girls', 'Nice Girls', 'Girlies', and 'Tomboys': Gender discourses, girls' cultures and femininities in the primary classroom," *Gender and Education*, vol. 13, no. (June 2001):153–167.

33 *Research from Duke University:* Ron Kaniel, Cade Massey, and David T. Robinson, "The Importance of Being an Optimist: Evidence from Labor Markets," working paper issued by National Bureau of Economic Research (website), September 2010. http://www.nber.org/papers/w16328.

35 *far more often than men:* Heidi Moore, "Little surprise here: women expected to do more at home—and at work," *The Guardian*, November 1, 2013. https://www.theguardian.com/commentisfree/2013/nov/01/women-work-harder-favors-never-counted.

38 Harvard Business Review *found that:* Tiziana Casciaro and Miguel Sousa Lobo, "Competent Jerks, Lovable Fools, and the Formation of Social Networks," *Harvard Business Review*, June 2005. https://hbr.org/2005/06/competent-jerks-lovable-fools-and-the-formation-of-social-networks.

39 *Research from the University of North Carolina, Chapel Hill:* J. P. Allen, M. M. Schad, B. Oudekerk, and J. Chango, "Whatever happened to the 'cool' kids? Long-term sequelae of early adolescent pseudo-mature behavior," *Child Development*, vol. 85, no. 5 (Sept-Oct, 2014): 1866–80. http://people.virginia.edu/~psykliff/Teenresearch/Publications_files/Allen%20Final%20Pseudomaturity%20Paper%20CD.2014.pdf.

3. SPEAK UP ASSERTIVELY
AND NICELY

42 *groundbreaking special report:* Katherine W. Phillips, "How Diversity Makes Us Smarter," *Scientific American*, October 1, 2014. https://www.scientificamerican.com/article/how-diversity-makes-us-smarter/.

43 *According to research by JoAnn Deak, Ph.D:* JoAnn Deak, Ph.D, qtd. in Jessica Ciencin Henriquez, "The Strange Phenomenon That's Preventing Girls From Reaching Their Dreams," *Teen Vogue*, January 8, 2016. http://www.teenvogue.com/story/girls-stop-camouflaging-build-self-esteem-confidence.

48 *more frequently than men:* Karina Schumann and Michael Ross, "Why Women Apologize More Than Men: Gender Differences in Thresholds for Perceiving Offensive Behavior," *Psychological Science*, vol. 21, issue 11 (September 2010): 1649–1655. http://journals.sagepub.com/doi/abs/10.1177/0956797610384150.

62 *by what you actually say:* Albert Mehrabian, *Silent Messages: Implicit Communication of Emotions and Attitudes* (Belmont, CA: Wadsworth), 1981.

63 *overly dominant or aggressive:* Marguerite Rigoglioso, "Researchers: How Women Can Succeed in the Workplace," Insights by Stanford Business (web-

site), March 1, 2011. https://www.gsb.stanford.edu/insights/researchers-how-women-can-succeed-workplace.

64 *In a 2017 article:* Susan Chira, "The Universal Phenomenon of Men Interrupting Women," *New York Times*, June 14, 2017. https://www.nytimes.com/2017/06/14/business/women-sexism-work-huffington-kamala-harris.html?_r=0.

4. GIVE FEEDBACK DIRECTLY
AND KINDLY

71 *A 2016 study from the University of Pennsylvania:* Birkan Tunc et al., "Establishing a link between sex-related differences in the structural connectome and behavior," *Philosophical Transactions of the Royal Society B: Biological Sciences*, volume 371, issue 1688 (February 19, 2016): web. Summarized in Penn Medicine News Release, February 9, 2016: https://www.pennmedicine.org/news/news-releases/2016/february/penn-medicine-quotbrain-road-m.

72 *According to David Rock:* Further explanation of David Rock's SCARF model can be found here: http://web.archive.org/web/20100705024057/http://www.your-brain-at-work.com:80/files/NLJ_SCARFUS.pdf.

76 *cells called mirror neurons*: J. M. Kilner and R. N. Lemon, "What We Currently Know About Mirror Neurons," *Current Biology*, Vol. 23, No. 23 (December 2, 2013): R1057-R1062. https://www.ncbi.nlm.nih.gov/pmc/articles/PMC3898692/.

80 *for every piece of criticism:* Jack Zenger and Joseph Folkman, "The Ideal Praise-to-Criticism Ratio," *Harvard Business Review*, March 15, 2015. https://hbr.org/2013/03/the-ideal-praise-to-criticism.

85 *for every piece of criticism:* Ibid.

5. MAKE DECISIONS FIRMLY
AND COLLABORATIVELY

91 *during times of stress:* Shelley E. Taylor et al., "Biobehavioral Responses to Stress in Females: Tend-and-Befriend, Not Fight-or-Flight," *Psychological Review*, Volume 107, No.3 (2000): 411–429). https://scholar.harvard.edu/marianabockarova/files/tend-and-befriend.pdf.

release more oxytocin: For example, Mara Mather, Nichole R. Lighthall, Lin Nga and Marissa A. Gorlick, "Sex differences in how stress affects brain activity during face viewing," *NeuroReport*, Volume 21, Issue 14 (October 6, 2010): 933–937. http://journals.lww.com/neuroreport/pages/default.aspx. Further reading about stress response in men and women can be found in: "Her Stress vs. His Stress—Women React Differently than Men to Pressure," Women's Brain Health Initiative (website), November 26, 2016. https://womensbrainhealth.org/better-thinking/her-stress-vs-his-stress-women-react-differently-than-men-to-pressure.

101 *similar role in the past:* Raina Brands and Isabel Fernandez-Mateo, "Women Are Less Likely to Apply for Executive Roles if They've Been Rejected Before," *Harvard Business Review*, February 7, 2017. https://hbr.org/2017/02/women-are-less-likely-to-apply-for-executive-roles-if-theyve-been-rejected-before.

In their book, Art & Fear: David Bayles and Ted Orland, *Art & Fear: Observations on the Perils (And Rewards) of Artmaking* (Santa Cruz, CA: The Image Continuum Press, 1993), p. 29.

6. NEGOTIATE WITH STRATEGY *AND* EMPATHY

109 *any time soon:* All data about women's earnings and the gender pay gap is from the American Association of University Women (AAUW), *The Simple Truth about the Gender Pay Gap* (report), published Spring 2017. http://www.aauw.org/research/the-simple-truth-about-the-gender-pay-gap/.

major cause of the wage gap: Corinne A. Moss-Racusin, John F. Dovidio, Victoria L. Brescoli, Mark J. Graham and Jo Handelsman, "Science faculty's subtle gender biases favor male students," *Proceedings of the National Academy of Sciences*, Volume 109, No. 41 (October 9, 2012): 16474–16479. http://www.pnas.org/content/109/41/16474.abstract#aff-1.

110 *In a 2014 study:* Marek N. Posard, "Status processes in human-computer interactions: Does gender matter?," *Computers in Human Behavior*, Volume 37 (May 2014): 189–195. Research brief prepared by Celeste Jalbert: http://www.rotman.utoronto.ca/FacultyAndResearch/ResearchCentres/GenderEconomy/Research/ResearchBriefs/RB08.

111 *chose to negotiate:* D. A. Small, M. Gelfand, L. Babcock, and H. Gettman, "Who goes to the bargaining table? The influence of gender and framing on the initiation of negotiation," *Journal of Personality and Social Psychology*, Volume 93, No. 4 (2007): 600–613. http://psycnet.apa.org/journals/psp/93/4/600/.

113 *In a 2011 study at Emory University:* Maura A. Belliveau, "Engendering Inequity? How Social Accounts Create vs. Merely Explain Unfavorable Pay Outcomes for Women," *Organization Science*, Volume 23, Issue 4 (July–August 2012): 1154–1174. http://pubsonline.informs.org/doi/pdf/10.1287/orsc.1110.0691.

studies out of Harvard and Carnegie Mellon: Hannah Riley Bowles, Linda Babcock, and Lei Lai, "Social incentives for gender differences in the propensity to initiate negotiations: Sometimes it does hurt to ask," *Organizational Behavior and Human Decision Processes* vol. 103 (2007): 84–103. https://www.cfa.harvard.edu/cfawis/bowles.pdf.

115 *better chance of success:* Hannah Riley Bowles and Linda Babcock, "How Can Women Escape the Compensation Negotiation Dilemma? Relational Accounts Are One Answer," *Psychology of Women Quarterly*, Vol. 37, Issue 1(2013): 80–96. http://journals.sagepub.com/doi/abs/10.1177/0361684312455524.

119 on behalf of *someone else:* Philipp Alexander Freund, Joachim Huffmeier, Jens Mazei, Alice F. Stuhlmacher, Lena Bilke and Guido Hertel, "A Meta-Analysis on Gender Differences in Negotiation Outcomes and Their Moderators," *American Psychological Association Psychological Bulletin*, Volume 141, No. 1 (2014): 85–104. http://www.apa.org/pubs/journals/releases/bul-a0038184.pdf. Summarized in APA Press Release, "Women Outperform men in Some Financial Negotiations, Research Finds," December 1, 2014: http://www.apa.org/news/press/releases/2014/12/financial-negotiations.aspx.

7. INVEST IN YOURSELF *AND* BE A TEAM PLAYER

138 *less goal-oriented approach to networking:* Athena Vongalis-Macrow, "Two Ways Women Can Network More Effectively, Based on Research," *Harvard Business Review*, November 26, 2012. https://hbr.org/2012/11/two-ways-women-can-network-more.

people of their own gender: Matthew Rothenberg, "It's Not Your Gender, It's Your Network," *The Ladders*, 2009. https://cdn.theladders.net/static/images/editorial/weekly/pdfs/your_network090930.pdf.

139 *as early as their male counterparts:* Herminia Ibarra, Nancy M. Carter, and Christine Silva, "Why Men Still Get More Promotions Than Women," *Harvard Business Review*, September 2010. https://hbr.org/2010/09/why-men-still-get-more-promotions-than-women.

9. MULTIPLY YOUR SUPERPOWER

171 *ever had a professional mentor:* Emily Jasper, "LinkedIn Report: Women without a Mentor," *Forbes*, October 25, 2011. https://www.forbes.com/sites/work-in-progress/2011/10/25/linkedin-report-women-without-a-mentor/#5c06a9e34ba7.

when you consider the research: Lillian T. Eby, Tammy D. Allen, Sarah C. Evans, Thomas Ng, and David DuBois, "Does Mentoring Matter? A Multidisciplinary Meta-Analysis Comparing Mentored and Non-Mentored Individuals," *Journal of Vocational Behavior*, Volume 72, No. 2 (2008): 254–267. https://www.ncbi.nlm.nih.gov/pmc/articles/PMC2352144/.

Index

About the Author

Fran Hauser is a long-time media executive, startup investor, and celebrated champion of women and girls. Fran funds and advises early-stage consumer-focused companies such as HelloGiggles, Mogul, The Wing, and Gem & Bolt. Sixteen of the nineteen companies in Fran's portfolio are founded by women, highlighting her broader commitment to increasing the representation of female founders.

Previously, Fran held President and General Manager positions at AOL, Moviefone, and Time Inc., where she played an integral role in building PEOPLE.com. She is also an advisor to 92Y Women in Power, Rent the Runway's Project Entrepreneur, WomenOne, and Girl Be Heard and serves on the board of directors of GlobalGiving.

Named one of the 6 Most Powerful Women in NYC's Tech Scene by Refinery29, Fran has appeared on CNBC and in *Forbes*, *Fast Company*, Vogue.com, Mashable, Ad Age, and more. She lives in Bedford, New York, with her husband and two sons.

Head over to www.nicegirlmyth.com to connect with Fran and read more about succeeding on your own terms.